THE WEATHER

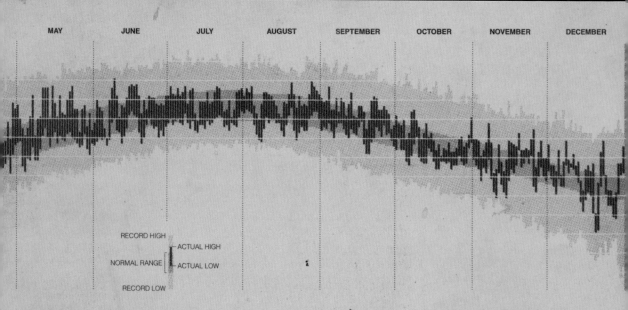

| MAY | JUNE | JULY | AUGUST | SEPTEMBER | OCTOBER | NOVEMBER | DECEMBER |

RECORD HIGH
— ACTUAL HIGH
NORMAL RANGE
— ACTUAL LOW
RECORD LOW

with normal monthly precipitation. Total precipitation was 51.96 inches, or 2.15 inches above normal. Total snowfall was 25.8 inches, or 3.4 inches above normal.

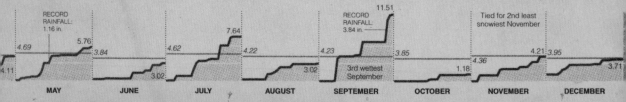

RECORD RAINFALL: 1.16 in.

4.69   5.76

4.11   3.84

3.02

4.62   7.64

4.22

RECORD RAINFALL: 3.84 in.

11.51

4.23   3.85

3rd wettest September

1.18

4.36   4.21   3.95

3.71

Tied for 2nd least snowiest November

| MAY | JUNE | JULY | AUGUST | SEPTEMBER | OCTOBER | NOVEMBER | DECEMBER |

kenneth goldsmith

"Repeating the current temperature . . ." The poet carefully transcribes radio transmissions such that a paragraph is a day, and a book is a year. Poet, documentarian, and archivist Kenneth Goldsmith has captured—exactly captured—the cadences of a voice that's even now droning inside your head.

There aren't and there are surprises. *The Weather* represents, after all, a year in which people in New York suddenly started paying attention to the weather in Baghdad.

There's no problem putting a voice with these words. The effect is a unison of read text and remembered voice, each paragraph a Cageian time bracket. Cheerful, alliterative, and full of commonsensical advice, the announcer increasingly resembles a poet with a gun to his head. "The battlefield forecast . . ."**—DAVID GRUBBS**

Kenneth Goldsmith is without a doubt the leading conceptual poet of this time. His poetry, which draws from Fluxus, Dada, and conceptual art traditions, is clever and self aware. With now classics such as *Fidget, Soliloquy,* and *Day,* he has made poetry out the mundane and when reading his work one is forced to reconsider the stakes and the measurements of aesthetic practice. *The Weather,* a collection of weather reports, is one more such test of poetry. And what is most striking about this book is how it aces the test. There is something wonderfully celebratory and shockingly pleasant and stimulatingly interesting about reading day after day of weather gone by.**—JULIANA SPAHR**

THE WEATHER

KENNETH GOLDSMITH

MAKE NOW

LOS ANGELES   2005

Published by Make Now Press, Los Angeles.

ISBN 0-9743554-2-9

FIRST EDITION

10 9 8 7 6 5 4 3 2 1

Interior and cover design by Karen Sheets.

Printed in Canada.

MAKE NOW
www.makenow.org

for Alan Licht

THE WEATHER

WINTER

couple of breaks of sunshine over the next couple of hours, what little sunshine there is left. Remember, this is the shortest day of the year. Looks like the clear skies hold off till later on tonight. It will be brisk and cold, low temperatures will range from twenty-nine in some suburbs to thirty-eight in midtown. Not a bad shopping day tomorrow, sunshine to start, then increasing clouds, still breezy, with a high near fifty. Couple of showers around tomorrow night, er, tomorrow evening, into early tomorrow night, otherwise partly cloudy later on, low thirty. For Monday, windy and colder with sunshine, a few clouds, high forty-two. And then for, er, Christmas Eve, mostly sunny, but with a chilly wind, high near forty degrees. For Christmas itself, cloudy with a chance for rain or snow, high thirty-six. Forty-three degrees right now and cloudy, relative humidity is fifty-five percent in midtown. Repeating the current temperature forty-three going down to thirty-eight in midtown.

Well, this is a very intense low and it's, uh, located just south of Jones Beach right now. It's going to be sliding off to the east, northeast, here as we, uh, go into the evening hours, but the radar is just loaded, uh, from the city back to the Delaware River. You actually have to get back to Allentown to find the end of the storm, but it's not going to be moving in any great hurry. We probably have a good four, five hours of good, steady snow, and at that time, it's going to be coming down hard, and, uh, therein lies, uh, the problem here because, uh, it's possible that, uh, the snow rate can be so heavy at times, we could easily pick up an inch or two in just one hour's time. So you've got a couple of hours of that and this, eh, one to three, eh, could be exceeded, uh, but right now we're looking for one to three in the city and Long Island, three to six in many of the western and northern suburbs, and even more than that further northwest. So just allow for some extra time to get around here this evening, it's gonna be quite messy for the next several hours. Things will start to improve after nine o'clock, it will be diminishing to flurries from west to east, probably all over by midnight. Stays very windy right on through the night, and then tomorrow will turn mostly sunny, uh, but still quite windy, with some gusts to forty and fifty miles an hour, a high of thirty-eight. Right now we have snowflakes and thirty-three, and a north wind at fifteen to twenty-five miles an hour. Repeating the current temperature thirty-three going down to thirty in midtown.

It'll be gusty and cold the rest of the day, but sunny for the most part, high temperature thirty-eight. Watch for a refreezing as the sun goes down, clear and cold tonight, diminishing wind, low twenty-four in many suburbs to thirty in midtown. Tomorrow sunny to partly cloudy high thirty-eight, then a little milder for the weekend, reaching forty-two Saturday with sunshine and forty-four on Sunday. No more storms until next week, and it may not snow again until next year. Currently winds out of the northwest at twelve, gusting to twenty-four miles per hour, relative humidity sixty-nine percent, thirty-two degrees in midtown heading for thirty-eight.

We're looking at a fair amount of sunshine as we go through the afternoon, temperatures though, staying on the chilly side, looking for a high of near forty degrees today. It's partly cloudy tonight, dry weather continues right through the weekend. We'll see a mix of clouds and sunshine for tomorrow, the high of forty degrees once again. Sunday begins a, um, warming trend, looking for a high of forty-four with partly sunny skies, also some sunshine for Monday, with a high up to forty-eight. New Year's Eve we're gonna get up near fifty degrees. Currently in Central Park, mostly sunny skies, thirty-five degrees, the humidity sixty-four percent, and the wind is northwest at seven miles an hour. Repeating the current temperature thirty-five headed up to forty in midtown.

Well, we are going to have a very tranquil weekend for the most part, uh, today, uh, sunshine, some clouds, up to around forty degrees. Uh, more clouds probably tomorrow, uh, there'll be a few flurries moving through the area later tonight and first thing tomorrow morning, not expecting to cause any problems but, uh, nonetheless, a couple of flurries passing by. Thirty-two for a low in midtown tonight, then tomorrow, temperatures again up near that forty degree mark, uh, for a high with, uh, wind picking up during the afternoon, so a little bit more uncomfortable tomorrow, from a temperature standpoint. On Monday, a limited amount of sunshine, high forty-two. More clouds for Tuesday, a breezy, milder day high fifty, watch out for some rain at night, especially if you're headed out to Times Square. Currently in Islip it's thirty, twenty-eight in Belmar, in Central Park it's thirty degrees under a partly sunny sky, the humidity at sixty-three percent, winds west at ten. Repeating the current temperature thirty degrees going up to forty in midtown.

Well, mostly clear skies, cold conditions for tonight. We're headed down to a low of thirty in midtown, twenty-two in many suburbs, then as sunshine shares the sky with some clouds tomorrow, we're headed up to a high of forty. More, in terms of clouds, move in tomorrow night, setting the stage for a cloudy day Tuesday, but a southwesterly breeze will bring in warmer air so, believe it or not, we're headed up to a high of fifty-two. It may shower on Tuesday, but more likely look for some rain Tuesday night for New Year's Eve celebrations, as well as for New Year's Day on Wednesday, the high Wednesday fifty. Forty-one, mostly cloudy, as we speak, in Central Park, the relative humidity fifty-seven percent, wind northwest at ten. Once again, forty-one headed down to thirty in midtown.

We have, uh, cloudy skies, uh, we'll see a few light showers, a touch of drizzle overnight, uh, temperatures will be staying, uh, well above the freezing mark. Watch, uh, going, well, north of the city, though, across, uh, Orange, uh, Putnam, into northern Fairfield County, uh, temperatures, uh, right around thirty, thirty-two degrees there, and there is, uh, a bit of icing taking place right now. And for tomorrow, mostly cloudy and milder, with a chance of a shower, high of fifty-two. Tomorrow evening, uh, looks like, uh, just a chance of an evening shower but, uh, as we get on toward midnight, uh, it looks like it'll be dry, uh, with, uh, temperatures, uh, around forty-three degrees at midnight in Times Square with a light northwest wind. Wednesday, New Year's Day, turning cloudy, uh, we will get into some steadier rain, probably late in the day or in the evening, and that will go, uh, right on into, uh, Thursday, high temperature on Wednesday forty-four. Right now we have forty degrees and a cloudy sky, with an east wind at six. Repeating the current temperature forty going down to thirty-five in midtown.

Well, we are looking at a, uh, cloudy, mild evening, also foggy, uh, especially on Long Island, uh, this is just the mild air coming on a southerly breeze off of the, uh, cold ocean which is, uh, causing, uh, that fog bank actually from the Verrazano Narrows bridge, all the way out to Long Island, and, uh, temperatures tonight will be staying in the forties. It'll be around forty-seven at midnight in Times Square, we may see a shower or two about that time as well, because there is going to be a cold front moving through during the middle of the night. And then tomorrow, uh, a storm on the southern end of that very same front, uh, is going to paying us a visit. So what is just going to be a shower, a bit of drizzle in the morning hours, uh, becomes a steady, cold, rain as we go through the day. Temperatures aren't gonna move much, uh, we'll stay in the lower forties, might even drop a bit in the afternoon. It's gonna get to be windy, the rain heavy at times tomorrow night, uh, even the possibility that we have, uh, some icing problems, uh, before it ends very late tomorrow night, the low temperature of thirty-two. Then on Thursday, cloudy, windy, uh, some left-over drizzle, the high of thirty-six. Right now we have fifty-two and mostly cloudy with a light west wind. Repeating the current temperature fifty-two going down to forty-two in midtown.

Um, I'm currently looking at the radar showing rain of a moderate intensity, in some cases continuing throughout the tri-state area. Our storm system right now is located off the Jersey Shore, and the general movement of these, well, they're not moving much at all. Eventually the precipitation will be lifting out to the north and east on Thursday morning, as will the storm, uh, but it's still quite a bit of rain to go, especially up in the Hudson Valley, Rockland, Westchester counties, northern New Jersey. And there are winter weather advisories in effect overnight for the, uh, potential for slick travel because of freezing rain and some sleet, so, not the nicest of nights, really anywhere, um. Union County, you're under a flood warning overnight so, um, a lot of melted snow and rain combined causing problems. We're going to get a break tomorrow by mid-morning, everything should be done, but it'll be a windy and cold day and then Friday, that's when our next storm system comes in, and it looks like it'll be a snow-producer that'll last into Friday night. Thirty-seven in midtown right now, relative humidity ninety-six percent, north wind at twelve miles per hour. It's raining and thirty-seven, heading down to thirty-two.

A cloudy, cold blustery day coming up today, uh, northerly winds, uh, bringing colder air into the region, and what makes that interesting is there's also another storm brewing, this one coming out of the southwest, uh, out of the middle of the country now, and we think that means snow will begin late tonight. It'll continue tomorrow, although probably change to rain and sleet for a while in the city and coastal areas, and then end tomorrow night. We think one to three inches of snow can accumulate, on average, across the metropolitan area. Go up to Interstate 287, three to six inches seems likely, and north of there, six inches or more. Saturday behind the storm, partly sunny, blustery, and chilly, with a high in the thirties. Right now it's thirty-two and cloudy in Central Park, temperature today going up only to thirty-five.

It's a messy start here, um, we've got, uh, quite a variety of conditions right now, ranging from just an all-out snowstorm in northwestern New Jersey into, uh, northern Westchester and Fairfield County, Connecticut, uh, but you get a little bit closer in, you find mixed precipitation, snow, sleet, even some freezing rain. And you get inside, uh, the Garden State Parkway into the city and out to Long Island, we're just dealing with a cold, wind-driven rain right now. Uh, this, uh, mix is going to be changing over to snow, from west to east, as we go through the night. Uh, in the city, though it's probably going to take until after midnight and, uh, at the same time, the storm is going to be, uh, almost, uh, over. So we're not not not looking at much in the way of an accumulation of snow in the city or on Long Island, maybe a coating to perhaps an inch, uh, but the further northwest you go, the more snow you are going to see and, uh, tra . . . uh, travel problems. Uh, temperatures, uh, in the city getting down around the freezing mark. And then for tomorrow, uh, this system will be up, uh, east of Boston by morning, uh, and then hustling away. All that's gonna be left here is a few morning flurries, otherwise a lot of clouds and a cold wind, thirty-six for a high, partly cloudy for tomorrow night. Sunday it clouds up once again with a high of thirty-six, and just a chance we could see a little bit of snow, or just some flurries late Sunday and Sunday night. Right now thirty-three with, uh, rain and a northeast wind at twenty-three miles per hour. Repeating the current temperature thirty-three going down thirty-two in midtown.

Well, it wasn't that bad of a storm in New York City proper and certainly not, eh, in south Jersey and on Long Island, in terms of snowfall or wintry precipitation. You go really north of Interstate 84, all the way up to Interstate 88 in New York State, and that's where all the damage is done, generally two, three feet of snow in that corridor. Most of it is done, we're still seeing on radar, a little bit of light snow in eastern parts of Westchester County and in Fairfield County, but accumulations are minimal. Just watch for slippery spots over the next couple of hours this afternoon, leftover clouds and a high of thirty-six. Tonight clearing, we'll get down to twenty-eight, so watch for icy spots, some of that slush refreezing in the suburbs. Tomorrow the clouds return, high thirty-six, and we may see a little light snow or flurries late tomorrow or tomorrow night. Then clouds and flurries for Monday, high thirty-eight, clouds and some sun Tuesday. At the moment, twenty-nine in White Plains, thirty-two in Islip, thirty-one with light snow in Central Park, relative humidity ninety-six percent, winds are out of the northwest at six miles an hour. Repeating the current temperature thirty-one going up to thirty-six in midtown.

And we are going to end up with some snow as we go through the afternoon and evening hours, uh, maybe it moves in sometime late this afternoon, and could go throughout the night tonight. A coating to an inch of snow is expected for most of the area with this event. Another storm moves through late tomorrow, into tomorrow night, and once again, brings a small amount of snow into the region. By Tuesday, flurries early in the day, windy with some sun in the afternoon. Wednesday and Thursday will be considerably milder with temperatures making it, uh, well, into the middle-and-upper-forties by Thursday. We are looking at temperatures again in the thirties at this point throughout most of the area. We're looking at about, oh, thirty exactly, in White Plains, thirty-three in Islip, and thirty-three in the Park, relative humidity is sixty-nine percent. Mostly sunny right now in New York City, thirty-three right now, we are going to go to thirty-six in midtown today.

Well, it's mostly light precipitation that, eh, we're seeing on the radar, and it is all in the form of snowfall, in spite of temperatures getting up above, uh, the freezing mark today, it's going to remain snow. But it is continuing to taper off, especially across north Jersey, and there's most likely going to be a few hours respite within the, uh, snowfall this afternoon. High temperature thirty-six degrees, most roadways just staying wet. What I'm cautious about is later on tonight, a cold front marches in from eastern Ohio, western Pennsylvania, temperatures dip back down below freezing, to a low of twenty-six degrees, so you get what's wet, freezing, and you get a covering to an inch of snowfall on top of that. Be cautious outside. Tomorrow windy and cold, clouds, sun, high thirty-two, RealFeel temperature is only in the teens, still windy Wednesday with a high of forty-two. Right now thirty-three Islip, thirty-two degrees, flurry action Central Park, going to thirty-six in midtown.

It's blustery and it's cold outside this morning, and it's going to remain that way throughout the day today, clouds and a few peeks of sun. The, uh, air temperature will not get above freezing, and when you weigh in the effect of the wind and the cloud cover, that RealFeel temperature is generally going to be in the teens. Tonight some milder air will begin, uh, to push toward the area. It will eventually make itself felt, but at first it will produce a period of snow tonight, a covering to an inch can occur, even in midtown, outside of the city, uh, an inch to maybe a couple of inches. Then tomorrow, turns partly sunny, windy and milder, up to forty. We'll take a run at fifty on Thursday, back to about forty on Friday, and then blustery and, uh, colder but, uh, dry over the weekend. Right now it is twenty-seven degrees and mostly cloudy in Central Park, the humidity is sixty percent, winds from the north at twelve, that makes the RealFeel temperature sixteen. Again the current temperature twenty-seven going up only to thirty-two.

And what we have here tonight is, uh, brisk conditions under partly to mostly cloudy skies, uh, relatively mild, uh, temperatures, uh, staying above freezing all across the region tonight, a low of thirty-eight in midtown. And a very mild day coming up tomorrow, partly sunny, windy, fifty in the afternoon. Enjoy it, it's going away, uh, cold air is going to be plunging in here tomorrow night and Friday, uh, Friday, once again, gusty winds but, uh, we will have the sun out, but a high temperature of only thirty-eight. And then we will step it down again over the weekend, lots of sunshine both Saturday and Sunday, but brisk and cold with a high both days around thirty degrees. Right now we still have forty-three, a cloudy sky with a west wind at eight. Repeating the current temperature forty-three going down to thirty-eight in midtown.

If you're a warm weather fan, today's your day, uh, but, uh, try to get out and enjoy it because it's not going to be repeated again for a while. It's windy today, that wind will be gusting frequently to thirty miles per hour, occasionally to near forty miles per hour. The temperatures will be up and above fifty in a lot of places, through the middle of the day and this afternoon. Tonight a cold front passes through, uh, temperatures drop into the thirties tonight, stay in the thirties tomorrow, despite sunny intervals. There'll be a gusty wind tomorrow also. As for the weekend, it'll be dry but cold. No worse than partly cloudy, high temperatures around thirty, thirty-two. Nighttime lows in the city down there, twenty, and down near ten in the colder suburbs. Right now it's forty-seven, cloudy in Central Park, temperature today going up to fifty.

For the football game on Sunday in Oakland it'll be cloudy, temperatures will be in the fifties. Could be a little bit of rain, uh, around the Oakland, San Francisco area as well. Around these parts, no rain and no snow in the forecast either, but plenty of cold. It'll be partly sunny, blustery today, the temperature slowly dropping, steady to slowly falling, probably down into the middle-thirties by the end of the day, into the low twenties tonight. The both days of the weekend are sunny but cold, with high temperatures only around thirty-two. Right now it's forty-one and partly sunny in Central Park, temperature today going down to thirty-six by evening.

Well, just a cold night in progress here, mostly clear skies. Uh, we'll start the day tomorrow with temperatures in the low to middle-twenties, and we'll see intervals of clouds and sunshine tomorrow with the wind picking up, and a frontal system, which is now in the upper Great Lakes, high around thirty-eight in the afternoon. That front will move through here quietly, skies will clear once again later tomorrow night, uh, windy, low twenties for an overnight low. And then just a blustery, colder day Tuesday with a good deal of sunshine, and a high of only twenty-eight degrees. Uh, we will be in the twenties again on Wednesday, clouds and some sun, brisk, maybe, eh, some flurries. Uh, there'll be another front moving through, and behind it, uh, a dry, cold day Thursday, with a high of thirty degrees. Currently we have twenty-seven in Islip, twenty-nine and clear in Central Park, a west wind at six. Repeating the current temperature twenty-nine going down to twenty-six in midtown.

We are locked into a cold weather pattern now that's going to last all week, and probably for the next couple of weeks. Every now and then we'll get a day like today, in which temperatures moderate modestly, we'll get up close to forty this afternoon, although there will be a gusty wind. Then a fresh batch of arctic air will arrive tonight and temperatures, by daybreak tomorrow, down to near twenty, with wind blowing, and despite sunshine tomorrow, for Wednesday we're only looking at high temperatures around thirty. So, continuously below freezing from tonight, uh, probably right into, if not through the day, on Thursday. It'll cloud up Thursday and there is a chance for some snow or flurries along about Friday. Right now it's twenty-six and partly cloudy in Central Park, humidity sixty-three percent, wind, uh, from the southwest at twelve, that makes the RealFeel temperature fifteen. Repeating the current temperature twenty-six going up thirty-eight.

Nice and sunny outside, but it's cold and it will remain cold for the rest of the day today, the rest of this week, and probably most of, if not all of, next week. Mostly sunny, though, for the rest of the day today, with a high about thirty. Then clear tonight, low twenty in the city, but down into the teens in the suburbs. Partly to mostly sunny, cold tomorrow, high near thirty. Increasing cloudiness Thursday, and there is a chance for a period of snow Thursday night into Friday morning. That's going to depend how far north the storm, uh . . . we do expect it to be in the southern states, if it decides to come northward, we'll certainly keep you posted. Right now it is twenty-three and mostly sunny in Central Park, temperature today going up to thirty.

Well, that four day forecast contains much of the same, just cold weather coming up, uh, for the foreseeable future. Right now, cloudy skies across the area, they're gonna stay mostly cloudy as we go through the overnight, temperatures drop off to twenty in midtown, teens in most suburbs. Then for the day on Wednesday, clouds can break for some sunshine at times, and there may be a couple of flurries as well, but temperatures can only manage the upper-twenties for our highs later on Wednesday afternoon, also only in the twenties on Thursday. Thursday is dry with sunshine, followed by increasing clouds, and then Friday morning, we may see a little bit of snow or flurries, but some sunshine returns for the afternoon, Friday's high twenty-eight. Right now it's cloudy and twenty-five in Central Park, the humidity fifty percent, and the wind is from the west at nine miles an hour. Again, the current temperature twenty-five, it'll go down to twenty in midtown.

Well, uh, on this Thursday morning, early we have a clear to partly cloudy sky and, of course, it's been cold, it is cold, it will continue to be cold, seems like forever. But, uh, the question now is snow, when will it occur, how much will we get? I think the amounts will be on the light side. Of course, what is the definition of that? An inch or less in the city, and perhaps upwards of three inches on eastern Long Island. When will it happen? Well, it should all get started about twenty-four hours from now, perhaps a little sooner than that. It's ba . . . basically gonna be a, uh, storm out over the Atlantic, which will be pointing some of its moisture in our direction late on this Thursday night and early Friday. We'll see that light snowfall, and the temperature heading down to nineteen in midtown this morning, later today, our high thirty. And it looks like Friday and Saturday, uh, temperatures will be in the upper-twenties as the cold air, uh, snow or no . . . that's a mainstay. Twenty-two in midtown right now, relative humidity fifty-five percent, the wind west ten miles per hour, making it feel like eleven. Clear and twenty-two heading down to nineteen.

Well, uh, right now the visibilities are up just a little bit, uh, two miles, for instance, at Newark and LaGuardia, uh, the snow coming down lightly. It was worse an hour ago, but visibilities have improved a little bit, and this is a sign, of course, that the, uh, snow is going to be much lighter, and letting up here over the next few hours. Uh, really I think, eh, whatever, uh, slippery conditions there have been, well, by the morning rush hour, they'll be gone because the roads will be treated definitely by then, so, uh, not much of an impact on the morning commute. Still, though, when all is said and done, most locations getting around an inch of snow. Later today we will see some sun, it will become windy after a low this morning of twenty-one, the high later today thirty-two. Very cold on this Friday night, the low fifteen in midtown. Uh, we haven't been fifteen in Central Park in over two years, and there will be lots of readings in the single digits in the suburbs. Looks like a cold weekend coming up, temperatures Saturday in the twenties. Right now twenty-three in midtown, the relative humidity ninety-six percent, light and variable winds, snowing lightly. Twenty-three, we're heading down to twenty-one.

Well, it's going to be moonlit for the first part of the night, but we're going to see the clouds increase, as a cold front heads eastward across, uh, Pennsylvania and New York, and eventually, uh, there could be some flurries breaking out as well, low sixteen in midtown, six in many of the suburbs. Any flurries should depart by the afternoon tomorrow, clouds, some sun, brisk and cold, the high of twenty-eight. Mainly cloudy tomorrow night with a low of twenty. A bit of snow or flurries to start on Monday, otherwise clouds and sun, high thirty-two. And for Tuesday and Wednesday, bitterly cold again, with some sunshine, high both days twenty-one. We're at twenty-one right now, humidity forty-five percent, under clear skies, the wind from the west at five miles per hour. Repeating the current temperature twenty-one going down to sixteen in midtown.

Well, more cold weather today, and also more cold weather for much of the upcoming week. Temperatures, uh, in the mid-and-upper-twenties for the most part right now, headed up to a high of twenty-eight degrees in midtown for the day today. We will see clouds and occasional sunshine, there may be a few flurries late tonight into tomorrow morning. Tonight, we're going to see temperatures drop down to between sixteen and twenty-two across the tri-state. Then for tomorrow, after the flurries move away, some sunshine with a cold, gusty wind, and a high of thirty degrees, lower twenties for highs Tuesday and Wednesday. Right now it's nineteen and mostly cloudy in Central Park, the humidity seventy-seven percent, and the wind is west at nine miles an hour. Again the current temperature nineteen, we'll go up to twenty-eight in midtown.

A cold afternoon it is, uh, the RealFeel readings right now between ten and fifteen. We have a fifteen to thirty mile-an-hour wind moving along and, uh, that wind will continue here this evening, and then drop off a little bit as we go through the rest of the night. But we're looking at cold weather here all week long. This is easily the coldest week of the winter so far, uh, maybe the coldest week that we're going to see as well. Uh, temperatures tonight, uh, dropping to fourteen, uh, and that's in Central Park but, uh, we will see some readings down around ten in many of the suburbs. Twenty-five tomorrow despite a lot of sunshine, uh, once again, uh, a pretty stiff wind, too, which will make it feel much lower than that. Uh, tomorrow night gets even lower, we're talking eleven in Central Park, uh, single digits every-where else. Wednesday, mostly sunny and only twenty-three, Thursday, cloudy to partly sunny, uh, mid, uh, twenties, and then on Friday, uh, a cold northwest wind, partly sunny skies the high only twenty-one. Right now we have twenty-nine under a partly sunny sky, northwest winds fifteen to thirty miles an hour. Repeating the current temperature, twenty-nine going down to fourteen in midtown.

Well, we have more cold weather in store coming up overnight, and also through the end of the week, we do stay cold, looking for a low of fourteen in midtown overnight, with clear to partly cloudy skies across the area. It is going to be staying rather windy as well, making it feel like it's near zero for much of the night. As we go through the day on Tuesday, we will see a good deal of sunshine, that gusty wind is going to continue, and we are going to see a very cold day with a high of twenty-five degrees, back down to eleven for a low Tuesday night, a mainly clear sky. Still lots of sunshine Wednesday, but more in the way of clouds on Thursday, highs in the lower to middle-twenties throughout the rest of the week. Currently in Central Park, partly cloudy and nineteen degrees, the humidity fifty-nine percent, and the wind is west at nine miles per hour, gusting to twenty, the RealFeel temperature nine. The current temperature nineteen headed down to fourteen in midtown.

Well, cold continues to be the headline weather story around these parts, and that's going to continue to be the case all week and into the weekend. It really . . . there really doesn't appear to be any significant moderation until sometime next week, but at least it will be sunny the rest of the day today, with the high in the middle-twenties. Clear and cold tonight, low, uh, about fourteen in the city, but down near zero in the interior cold spots. Mostly sunny tomorrow, high again in the middle-twenties. Clouds and sun Thursday, with a couple of flurries a possibility. It looks like Thursday and Friday are probably the coldest days of the week, with highs in the low twenties, and then sunny and cold on Saturday, with a high of twenty-five. Right now it's seventeen and sunny in Central Park, humidity's fifty-six percent, wind from the west at ten, makes the RealFeel temperature nine. Repeating the current temperature seventeen going up to twenty-five.

Yeah, it's definitely another bundle-up-before-you-step-outside, uh, morning, uh, sunshine not going to be very effective today, uh, the temperature only into the middle-twenties, as our string of days of, uh, freezing and below continues. Tomorrow probably even colder, we don't look for temperatures to get out of the teens tomorrow, and there'll be a wind blowing, that RealFeel temperature will be below zero much of the day tomorrow, there may be a couple snow flurries, especially tomorrow afternoon and night. Friday, it's still cold but sunny, windy, high of twenty-five. Sun, less wind, but still cold Saturday, and then Sunday we may get all the way up to thirty-two. Next week we should get above freezing, but right now it's thirteen and mostly sunny in Central Park, humidity sixty-one percent, wind from the west at fifteen, makes the RealFeel temperature four below zero. Repeating the current temperature thirteen going up to twenty-five.

Well, it continues to be extremely cold, uh, this morning. The sun is up but it's not helping a whole lot. We only expect readings to be in the teens this afternoon, the wind will gust to between twenty and thirty miles an hour, and that will make that the RealFeel temperature well below zero. Tonight the temperature doesn't drop a whole lot, but the wind stays up so it's going to continue to feel extremely cold. And tomorrow will be cold and windy, but the sun will help out a little bit more tomorrow, up to twenty-seven. About thirty with less wind and sunshine on Saturday, and then increasing cloudiness on Sunday. Right now it is ten mostly sunny in Central Park, humidity is sixty-three percent, wind from the northwest at ten, that makes the RealFeel temperature zero. Repeating the current temperature ten, going up only to eighteen.

It's a bitterly cold morning out there. That's nothing new it's, uh, very similar to the way it was yesterday, RealFeel temperature right now minus eleven. We're in frostbite territory. It's going up to twenty-seven, though, this afternoon, some relief, but still, very cold. Tonight, going to to twenty in midtown, ten to fourteen in many suburbs. Tomorrow sunshine, temperature inching up toward thirty-two. We have a shot at thirty-four to thirty-six degrees on Sunday before the next cold front arrives. Flurries, or a period of snow late, Sunday or Sunday night into early Monday, and then partly sunny late Monday, high twenty-six. It's eight degrees, relative humidity fifty-seven percent, winds out of the west northwest at thirteen, gusting to seventeen, the RealFeel temperature minus eleven, the temperature eight heading to twenty-seven.

Well, uh, I'm looking at, uh, current radar, and it's still showing some of the light snow occurring in the city, and especially out on central and eastern Long Island. Uh, as you look to the west, though, across northern parts of New Jersey, this is beginning to taper off now, it's just a few flurries, for instance, in Morris County and Sussex County. Uh, this all associated with the leading edge of a bitterly cold air mass, of course, um, really much of this month, we've had temperatures below normal, but you haven't seen nothin' yet. Uh, looks like our temperatures tomorrow will be in the teens, we're headed down to thirteen in midtown overnight, and RealFeel temperatures tomorrow, when you factor in the wind, they will be below zero. So, uh, basically we're spending the, uh, entire day tomorrow, albeit a sunny day, between thirteen and eighteen degrees. Very cold tomorrow night, temperatures moderate somewhat Tuesday and Wednesday, we could have a rain or snow shower. Right now twenty-nine in midtown, relative humidity ninety-two percent, the air calm. It's snowing lightly and twenty-nine, we're heading down to thirteen.

It's exceptionally cold this morning, twelve degrees in Central Park, the wind is, uh, gusting, that RealFeel temperature is near zero. It's a pretty-looking morning, and it will be a nice-looking day with sunshine, but that sun is gonna be rather ineffective as temperatures will only be in the teens this afternoon, and the wind will continue to be gusty. Tonight will be clear and very cold, with a low of eight, but down near, and even below zero, interior sections. We could have a five or eight below zero somewhere in some of the, uh, snow-covered areas north of the city. Sunshine tomorrow, less wind, it will feel better in the afternoon with a high in the twenties, and mostly cloudy on Wednesday, moderating up to thirty-seven, and maybe there's a little bit of either snow or rain. Right now it is twelve degrees, mostly sunny in Central Park, northwest wind at eleven, that makes the RealFeel temperature zero. Repeating the current temperature twelve going up only to eighteen today.

Temperatures today are going to moderate, albeit slowly because of cloud cover. That cloud cover could produce a snow flurry today, but the temperatures should get into the low to middle-twenties later in the day, and then not drop very much tonight, might not drop, uh, below twenty in most places, but there'll also be, uh, a little enhancement in some snow tonight, not a big storm, but there could be a covering to a fresh inch, or at most two, by the time it ends tomorrow morning. Clouds linger the rest of the day tomorrow, but temperatures moderate into the thirties. Thursday will be mostly sunny, cold about thirty-two, and then increasing cloudiness on Friday. Right now it's twelve and cloudy in Central Park, temperature today going up to twenty-six.

Well, uh, our radar continuing to show light snow scattered around the metropolitan area right now, uh, there are breaks in the snow pattern, but it extends all the way back into, uh, central and western Pennsylvania. So we've got several hours yet in which there will be intermittent light snow, certainly not piling up, uh, an inch or probably less in Manhattan and across most of the five boroughs, but there might be a little bit more than an inch, uh, on, in some areas, uh, west and to the southwest of the city. All in all, a light kind of a snowfall, and the important thing is that the cold is nowhere near as intense as it's been. With clearing tonight, we look for low in twenties. A partly sunny day tomorrow, high thirty-four, up to thirty-six Friday, chance for some rain or snow late Friday night into Saturday. Right now twenty-nine degrees, cloudy, there is some snow around the area, uh, in midtown, the temperature today going up to thirty-six.

Well, we're going to see mainly clear skies now as we go through the overnight, lows going down to around twenty-two degrees. Then for the day Thursday, we have some sunshine coming up, and a high goes to thirty-four degrees in the afternoon. It won't be quite so cold as we get into the weekend, Friday's high is thirty-eight as clouds increase, looking at temperatures going into the forties for both Saturday and Sunday afternoon. On Saturday, we may see a bit of rain or snow, Sunday is dry with some sunshine. Right now it's clear and thirty degrees in Central Park, the humidity seventy-eight percent, and the air is calm. Again the current temperature thirty, we'll go down to twenty-two in midtown.

Ah, yes, indeedy, and actually it's a . . . uh, you know . . . fairly tranquil as well, with sunshine getting dimmed by high mid-level clouds, high temperature thirty-four degrees. Clouds easily thicken tonight, low thirty. That's the easy part of the forecast. The question mark is whether or not the, uh, rain that's currently over the Delmarva Peninsula will actually come this far north, or will it get to a certain point over central Jersey, then pivot offshore? It's gonna be a close call, we could see a little bit of light flurry action or freezing drizzle first thing tomorrow morning, if that precipitation's here. In a best case scenario, it doesn't do anything until tomorrow afternoon, and by that point, it would just be rain and drizzle, with a high of thirty-eight degrees, but watch out for air and dense fog. A secondary storm system on Saturday brings in rain or wet snow, with a high near forty. Right now it's thirty in Caldwell, thirty degrees and partly sunny in Central Park, headed up to thirty-four in midtown.

Well, uh, of course, uh, T.G.I.F., uh, that applies to the work week but, uh, not so really in terms of the weather, which will be going downhill later on today. We've got clouds now, thirty-two in midtown. Well, the temperature at daybreak should be, in most places, between twenty-eight and thirty-two. Now it'll be later this morning, probably around ten or eleven o'clock, we'll start to see a little bit of light rain and snow breaking out. I think that by the afternoon rush hour, it's just going to be plain rain in the city, but again as you go farther north and west, especially north and west of I-287, could see a, uh, wintry mix, uh, but everything should go over to plain rain, if not late on this Friday night and early Saturday. Once we get this wet weather out of the way, we're going to be treated to temperatures in the forties. Remember, the last time it was forty in midtown was back on the thirteenth of this month. We should start off February with a high of forty, going up to forty-eight, we think, by Monday. Right now thirty-two in midtown, the relative humidity sixty-four percent, wind northeast five miles per hour, cloudy and thirty-two, we're going down to near twenty-eight.

Well, we have a damp Friday afternoon ahead and, uh, some rain and drizzle in spots. There have been a few sleet pellets recently but, uh, it should be well above freezing, so no problems for travel, a high of thirty-eight. Now tonight, periods of rain, and that will be for tomorrow as well, low tonight thirty-four, high tomorrow forty. However, a winter weather advisory, where the rain will mix with ice and snow, northwest of Interstate 287, could be a coating to an inch there. It'll turn out partly sunny, up to forty-four Sunday, and then Monday sun followed by clouds, breezy, mild with a high of forty-eight. Right now we have some light rain, a few sleet pellets in Central Park, thirty-four degrees, the humidity ninety-two percent, the wind northeast at six. Repeating the current temperature, thirty-four headed up to thirty-eight this afternoon.

Well, we are looking at clouds and some sunshine today, and we're also looking at an area of rain which is in eastern Pennsylvania now, and looks like it's, uh, tending to shrink as it comes eastward, but it's certainly gonna move into northwest New Jersey within the next hour, and I think there will be some rain in areas north and west of Interstate 287 today. There certainly could be a shower in parts, and other parts, of the metropolitan area, but a mild day getting up to around fifty, highs tomorrow in the forties, with a mix of clouds and sun. And, most importantly, it's Groundhog Day eve, just one day before the big holiday and, uh, the weather today looks like it's going to be just fine. Clouds, there's a slight chance of a slight sprinkle this morning, but there will also be sunshine, and the temperature getting into the forties. Tomorrow there may be a couple of hours of either wet snow or rain as a cold front passes through. Right now, cloudy, forty-four in Newark, forty-three in Central Park, winds out of the east at six miles per hour. Repeating the current temperature forty-three going up to forty-eight in midtown today.

Now Staten Island Chuck did not see his shadow, meaning that Spring is, uh, getting ready to spring. But of course, Punxsutawney Phil did see his shadow, indicating six more weeks of winter. We've also heard from, uh, from, uh, Buckeye Chuck out in Ohio, and he agrees with Staten Island Chuck, and they're against old Punxsutawney Phil. So, uh, we've got battling groundhogs here, and I guess time will tell, as it usually does. As far as weather is concerned, another mild day today, but then it turns colder tonight, there can be some rain and snow this afternoon and evening, maybe a few hours' worth. At this point, we are not anticipating any snow accumulation, but it will be a whole heck of a lot colder tomorrow, despite sunshine, high temperatures tomorrow will only be in the thirties, and maybe not too far into the thirties at that. Right now we're thirty-three degrees in midtown, headed down to twenty-two tonight.

Well, uh, on this Tuesday morning, we still have a temperature of forty degrees in midtown, uh, we're not expecting the temperature to change all that much here over the next few hours. We have clouds, the radar showing a bit of rain going on across the, uh, Hudson Valley and in Connecticut. Later on today, uh, that radar will be filling in throughout the tri-state area, I think after five a.m., and, uh, we'll be seeing periods of rain right through the morning rush hour on into, uh, midday. Probably the rain will be wrapping up around twelve noon or one o'clock, uh, but we're to be, uh, undergoing some big temperature changes here. It should rise to fifty-two later on today, with a mild southwesterly wind, and then the rain stops. Drier and much colder air will be rushing in later this afternoon, temperatures, probably winding up near forty by the afternoon rush. We're headed all the way down to twenty-eight on this Tuesday night, and we'll stay cold and mainly dry the rest of the week, other than for a flurry on Friday, I don't expect much to happen, temperatures will be in the lower and middle-thirties. Right now forty in midtown, the relative humidity seventy percent, the wind south, six miles per hour. Cloudy and forty, heading down to thirty-nine.

It's going to be windy and cold today, uh, that wind gusting still close to thirty miles an hour at times, uh, and actually are one or two little very light snow flurries scattered around, but there will also be ample sun today, with a high in the middle-thirties. Clear tonight, a low twenty-four in the city, teens in the suburbs. Sun followed by clouds tomorrow, and there's a chance for a period of snow tomorrow night into Friday morning, if it materializes. It doesn't look like a major storm, but there will be a pretty important storm along the middle Atlantic coast Friday morning that we're going to have to keep a watch out on. Then clearing later Friday, the weekend looks dry and chilly. Thirty-one degrees now and partly sunny in Central Park, temperature today going up to thirty-six.

Well, we are not going to see any weather troubles for the Thursday morning rush hour, but the Friday morning rush hour could bring a very different story. Clouds are going to be increasing as we go into the day on Thursday, then Thursday night into Friday, we're going to be watching low pressure, uh, swinging up the mid-Atlantic coast. It's going to be throwing some snow our way. Looks like overnight Thursday night, into the first half of Friday, is going to be our snow chance, and there can be a couple of inches on the ground by the time this storm is all said and done later Friday afternoon. We'll dry out, though, on Saturday, mostly sunny skies, the high thirty-four, but there could be a bit of snow and flurries again by the end of the day Sunday. Right now twenty-six and clear in Central Park, the humidity forty-two percent, and the wind is from the west at nine miles an hour. Again the current temperature twenty-six, it'll go down to twenty-four in midtown.

About two inches of snow on the ground in Central Park now, three to four inches of snow, uh, just about everywhere else, and looking at our radar now, heavy snow covering the metropolitan area. It's gonna stay that way for at least the next few hours, probably until around noon, it'll snow at the rate of a half-an-inch to an inch per hour, and that means we think we'll wind up with a pretty solid average of six inches across the metropolitan area, a little less than that, of course right, in midtown Manhattan, a little less to the north, a little more to the east and to the south, six to ten inches worth out toward the, uh, Nassau and Suffolk County, uh, line, and also in Hunter and Somerset and Middlesex and Monmouth Counties in central New Jersey. Snow ends early-to-midafternoon, it'll be clear tonight, sunny tomorrow, high of about thirty-two, clouding up Sunday with a chance for some snow on Monday. Right now, twenty-eight degrees and snowing in Central Park, with the temperature today going up to thirty-two.

Feels pretty quiet across the country this evening. We do have a front, uh, draping from Michigan back into the Central Plains, and curling back up into the northern Rockies. Also a low over the southern Rockies is generating some rain and mountain snow. We may eventually have to deal with that one, uh, come Monday, but for the rest of the weekend it's just dry, cold weather. We'll have, uh, temperatures in the teens tonight, to around twenty in midtown, thirty-eight tomorrow under partly sunny skies. And then that system from the southwest, uh, runs over to the southeastern states, and then up the eastern seaboard, and likely to deliver a little bit of snow here on Monday, uh, with a high temperature around thirty-four. Behind it, another shot of some very cold air. Tuesday and Wednesday it's going to be blustery, uh, we will have some sunshine both days, but temperatures only in the twenties. Right now twenty-eight and a clear sky, with a southwest wind at nine. Repeating the current temperature twenty-eight going down to twenty in midtown.

Yeah, well, things are relatively quiet right now, though we're going to be seeing an increase in those clouds as we go through the afternoon, and into the nighttime hours. High this afternoon thirty-six, low tonight twenty-eight. Then by tomorrow morning an area of low pressure off the Carolina coast will throw some snow our way. Snow may arrive at some point during the morning, perhaps between seven and nine a.m., and continuing into the afternoon, accumulating a general one to three inches, possibly, uh, a few higher spots, uh, a few higher amounts, I should say on eastern Long Island, high thirty-four. Tons of clouds and sun for Tuesday and Wednesday, it'll be windy and cold each day, the high Tuesday twenty-five, and on Wednesday there could be a few flurries, high twenty-eight. Thirty-five with some sunshine in Central Park, humidity forty-five percent, the wind west at fourteen, gusting to twenty miles an hour. Repeating the current temperature thirty-five going up to thirty-six in midtown.

There's a low pressure area on the North Carolina coast, another one coming from the Ohio Valley, and the two should combine to give us snow during the afternoon hours, most of it falling between about two or three this afternoon, and seven and eight this evening, so the evening commute is the target time for most of the trouble. And the first snow will simply melt on the streets, and the reason is that it's well above freezing right now. We're expecting one to two inches when all is said and done by late this evening around the city, two to four inches in many suburbs, as much as six, perhaps, on eastern Long Island, because the storm will be strengthening as it moves away from the coast. The temperature steadier, slowly falling this afternoon, it should be down to thirty-two degrees by four or five p.m., then down to twenty-four tonight. Tomorrow's high twenty-eight, then blustery and cold Wednesday and Thursday, the high Wednesday twenty-eight, only twenty-four on Thursday. Currently in midtown thirty-six degrees, relative humidity fifty-nine percent, winds out of the south, southeast at eight miles per hour. Thirty-six degrees in midtown, heading slowly down this afternoon.

Well, we're looking, uh, partly to mostly cloudy skies tonight, uh, we'll see some flurries here a little later on this evening. There's actually a pretty good area of snow coming through central Pennsylvania at the moment. It should weaken a bit as it approaches us but, uh, we could, uh, see a dusting of snow here a little bit later on. Uh, that will probably stop only to renew again, uh, toward daybreak as an arctic cold front arrives on the scene, a low temperature of around twenty degrees. Uh, flurries tomorrow morning, maybe even a heavier snow squall as that boundary moves through, and then the rest of the day, a cold wind with some sunshine, a high of thirty. Uh, just a windy bitterly cold night coming up tomorrow night, clear to partly cloudy skies, temperatures in the upper single digits to around ten, but it's gonna feel like it's well below zero. Thursday partly sunny, brisk and quite cold, a high only twenty-two. Right now we have twenty-four, a partly cloudy sky, with a northwest wind at six. Repeating the current temperature twenty-four going down to twenty in midtown.

The, uh, story of, uh, afternoon weather, in fact, the weather right through tomorrow, is that the wind is going to make these temperatures that are cold anyway, feel even colder as this arctic air pours into the region, uh, behind this morning's arctic front. We'll see intervals of sun this afternoon, temperatures will slowly fall, twenty-five by day's end, but the winds gusting up to forty will bring our RealFeel temperature down to near or below zero by the evening rush. Same story tonight, bitterly cold, ten in midtown, single digits in the suburbs. Brisk, very cold, only twenty-two for a high tomorrow, could see some snow then by the weekend. Right now it's partly sunny, thirty-one in Central Park, humidity forty-one percent, a west wind gusting to thirty-one, gives us our RealFeel temperature of about nineteen. Repeating the current temperature thirty-five and it's going down to twenty-five.

Clear, brisk and very cold overnight, uh, we'll reach, uh, fourteen in midtown, ten, maybe eight degrees in some of the suburbs. And then a partly sunny day tomorrow, with afternoon temperatures around thirty degrees, a little lighter wind now that the high will be on the eastern seaboard. Uh, the next, uh, system we have to tangle with is a big storm which is, uh, causing precipitation over much of the West, actually all the way from California, now spreading out into the, uh, mid-Mississippi Valley. And, uh, we do expect to see some snow to come in here around or shortly after midnight tomorrow night, and go into Saturday morning, we could pick up to, uh, two, to perhaps, four inches accumulation. And then Saturday afternoon, and Saturday night, into Sunday morning, cloudy, windy and cold, temperatures will be in the twenties, and we can see some snow once again, Sunday afternoon and Sunday night. Right now eighteen and a clear sky, with a northwest wind at six. Repeating the current temperature temperature eighteen going down to fourteen in midtown.

The clouds are going to be building as we head for the early part of tonight, and by later tonight, some snow could arrive, our low down to eighteen degrees. Snow amounts will generally be on the light side. It could cause some problems if you're going to be traveling tomorrow morning, um, as much as an inch, but a lot of places see just a dusting. Later tomorrow brisk and quite cold, clouds should give way to some sunshine, the high twenty-three. Mainly clear, brisk and very cold tomorrow night, low ten in midtown, single digits in the suburbs. And clouds return on Sunday, and we could have some snow arriving later in the day or at night, and this time it could be a more significant storm. Details are still sketchy at this point, you'll want to keep it tuned right here. High twenty-two degrees, windy and cold on Monday, some snow or flurries possible through the morning hours, and clearing in the afternoon, the high thirty-two. Twenty-nine and mainly cloudy in Central Park, the wind from the west at about nine miles an hour, and the RealFeel temperature twenty. Current temperature once again twenty-nine headed down to eighteen in midtown.

And we see a little sunshine popping out of the clouds this afternoon. Overall not that bad of an afternoon, a couple of spots a little windy, actually at JFK winds, uh, north at seventeen miles an hour, gusting to twenty-two miles an hour right now. We are going to see some inclement weather as we go through the morning, now, clouds do increase tomorrow, that's in advance of a storm that will bring six to twelve inches of snow later tomorrow night, and into the day Monday. By Tuesday and Wednesday, things start to warm up a little bit, we should see a little sun as well. Twenty-four at Newark, twenty-four at LaGuardia, and twenty-three in the Park, cloudy in New York, relative humidity fifty-two percent, wind north at nine miles an hour gusting to twenty-two miles an hour. Twenty-three now, we'll go to twenty-six this afternoon.

And what a forecast it is too as we're, uh, hearing here the snow is starting to fly around the region. Uh, it will become steady, uh, over the next couple of hours, and inch its way northward through the, uh, tri-state area. Uh, the storm is a very slow moving system, we're looking at probably snow in the air for at least the next thirty hours, which is why we're talking about so much snow and, uh, part of the problem too is the fact that it is so cold, uh, with temperatures only in the teens right now and, uh, they will slowly rise up into the middle-twenties, uh, but we're easily looking at easily a foot to a foot and a half of snow. There is potential for a couple of feet, uh, before it finally tapers off around midnight tomorrow night, uh, we'll probably have three to six inches on the ground by the morning rush hour, and around a foot by the evening rush hour. So it's going to be tough getting around here tomorrow. In addition to the snow on the ground, we're gonna have a lot of blowing and drifting, because we're gonna look at a very strong northeast wind, uh, poor visibility during the height of the storm. And then on Tuesday, uh, clouds may even break for a little bit of sunshine, thirty-two degrees for a high. Fifteen and cloudy right now, a north wind at six. Repeating the current temperature fifteen and temperatures, uh, steady and or slowly rising in midtown tonight.

It continues to snow hard, uh, very hard in parts of the metropolitan area, and looking at the radar, there's more heavy snow from here southwest all the way down to the Chesapeake Bay area, and that snow has got to come northeastward, so we're going to continue to get snow falling at the rate of an inch to two inches per hour from now, probably, until early afternoon, maybe two to three o'clock. And that means that we could get another four to six or in some places, even eight inches of new snow on top of what we've already got. The storm total in Central Park will wind up pretty close to twenty inches or so, with some places winding up with, uh, probably over two feet, and then you've got to add in the drifts caused by the thirty to forty mile-an-hour winds. It will end this evening, tomorrow turning partly sunny, up to about thirty-two. By Thursday it will be up forty, but right now it's twenty degrees and snowing, the temperature today only going up to twenty-six.

Well, uh, partly cloudy skies here for the rest of the night, high teens in the suburbs, uh, for an overnight low to, uh, twenties in the city. And we will have a decent day tomorrow, uh, a dry one with sunshine followed by clouds, upper-thirties in the afternoon. The next, uh, frontal system is, uh, a relatively weak one now, causing some flurries out in Wisconsin, uh, down into the Chicago area, that'll be passing through here tomorrow evening. Uh, we can see a, uh, few flurries or sprinkles, and then it will clear late tomorrow night. Some nice weather, then, Thursday and Friday behind that front, milder actually, lots of sunshine, Thursday forty-four, Friday sunshine followed by clouds, the high of forty-six, and then a shot of rain Saturday, with temperatures in the forties. Thirty-two and partly cloudy with, uh, a light north to northwest wind.

Repeating the current temperature thirty-two going down to twenty-six in midtown.

We're gonna get a break in the weather, not only for today but for the next, uh, well, three days as clouds, uh, thin out for partial sunshine today. We'll get the temperature up close to forty this afternoon, certainly above freezing and well into the thirties. Might be a sprinkle or flurry this evening then clearing tonight. Tomorrow a mostly sunny day. I'll tell ya, if you're outside tomorrow afternoon, there won't be much of a breeze, the sun will be out, temperatures into the forties, it will feel good. And then a, uh, nice day Friday but increasing clouds. Rainy and windy Saturday, and that combination of rain and melting snow can cause street and highway flooding Saturday. Dry Sunday but blustery and colder. Right now it's thirty-two and partly sunny in Central Park, temperature today going up to thirty-eight.

Uh, yes and, uh, gee, where have you heard a cold forecast before? I think, uh, basically this entire winter, uh, really exceeded our expectations, or maybe last winter was just so darn mild, uh, that you wanted to believe, uh, winters would stay this way forever. Well, we've got arctic air tonight, some clouds, thirty-four in midtown, we're heading down to twenty-four. We'll be hard pressed to get, uh, close to the freezing mark tomorrow, looking like thirty, thirty-one degrees, with some sunshine and a brisk wind. Now, tomorrow night when that wind dies down, we're going down to the teens, about thirteen in midtown, single digits in many suburbs. A cold and dry pattern takes us through mid-week, but the storm system organizing in the southern states, where have you heard that before?, uh, will be providing us with some precipitation Thursday, Thursday night, early Friday and much of that will be in the form of snow. How much? A little too early to tell. Right now thirty-four in midtown, relative humidity fifty-nine percent, the wind light and variable. It's cloudy and thirty-four, heading down to twenty-four.

Our cold weather continues, and despite sunshine today, the temperature won't get above thirty-two in most places, and it'll drop down into the teens throughout tonight, single digits in many suburbs. Tomorrow, uh, kind of a mix of clouds and sun but, uh, by the time we get to Thursday, it'll be cloudy and we've, uh, got snow again in the forecast later Thursday, Thursday night, into Friday morning. This next storm still way out into southern California, so it's got a long ways to come, and we've still got a lot of time to watch it. It's not going to be the kind of a storm like the President's Day blizzard, but it could be a formidable storm, enough snow to get the shovels and plows out again, and we'll keep you posted.

Right now twenty-eight and sunny in Central Park, temperature today going up to thirty-two.

Uh, it's that old Christmas song "Let It Snow, Let It Snow," not so this afternoon. A lot of cloud cover, twenty-six degrees but, see, this is just one piece of our latest storm system. It's actually going to move farther away tonight, so the clouds part company, low fifteen to twenty, then the clouds quick to return tomorrow, with the high near thirty degrees. It's shortly after midnight tomorrow night, through the first part of Friday afternoon, that we'll have that accumulation, most areas, at least from the, uh, nearby suburbs, from the city on eastward across Long Island, three to six inches. North of the city, it'll be one to three inches and that's probably a similar, uh, bet, uh, north of I-80 as well, but once get on into, uh, central Monmouth County on southward, it could be as much as six to ten inches worth of snow. I got my shovel. It's sixteen this hour, White Plains twenty with clouds, going to twenty-six in midtown.

Well, if this were a baseball game, we might call this a, uh, swing and a miss. Uh, this is a pretty good storm, but most of it's going to be passing us by to the south. It's been snowing most of the day down across Washington, Baltimore and getting into, uh, the southern half of New Jersey, and that corridor is looking at a good half-a-foot, some places as much as eight inches, before it tapers off tomorrow morning. Uh, but the northern fringe of it is having a hard time making its way up through New Jersey, but eventually we are going to see some snowflakes in the pre-dawn hours, uh, but it's not gonna last long. It'll, uh, continue on through the morning, but will taper off to flurries again during, by lunchtime, and we may have to scrape together the snow to get up to an inch, uh, we're calling for one to three. Of the three, I think it's definitely more likely south of the city. Temperatures will be in the middle-twenties to start the day, thirty-four in the afternoon. Over the weekend, upper-thirties to near forty both days, uh, Saturday a little bit of sunshine, Sunday looks to be a cloudy day, we may even see a bit of wet snow or rain. Currently thirty degrees and cloudy with the northeast wind at nine. Repeating the current temperature thirty going down to twenty-six in midtown.

Well, two things we know about this weekend, one, we're not going to have the big washout like we did last weekend, and two, cold air is going to be held at bay, for now. It will be arriving here with a vengeance on Sunday night, as an arctic cold front moves through, and temperatures, therefore, Monday will be no higher than about thirty-three. Tuesday will be even worse but, eh, Monday and Tuesday, well, that's still a long way off we hope, uh, let's enjoy the weekend and moderate temperatures. Temperature thirty-three right now, heading down to twenty-eight, clouds will limit sun later today, but still not all that bad with a high of thirty-eight. There'll be a few showers with rain and wet snow, especially on this Saturday night and early Sunday. Sunday's high actually will be forty-two, but then that much colder air moves in, and as I gave you the details earlier, Monday and Tuesday, lower thirties. Thirty-three right now, relative humidity seventy-two percent, light and variable wind, cloudy, thirty-three, heading down to twenty-eight.

Well, we've got a little bit of everything here, uh, over the next forty-eight hours. Uh, at the moment, uh, we have an area of, uh, both rain and wet snow breaking out from the Pennsylvania and upstate New York, uh, some flakes have been, uh, on occasion, across Sussex and Orange county, uh, they might even pick up, uh, an inch of slushy snow there before it goes over to rain very, very late tonight. In closer to the city, we do expect to see a bit of rain at times here tonight, uh, there could be some wet snowflakes mixed in as well, at least though midnight or two in the morning, and then it's, uh, too mild aloft to support anything frozen, a low temperature of thirty-five. Tomorrow though, it's periods of rain and drizzle for everybody, forty-four for a high temperature. That'll come to an end tomorrow evening, then it's a shot of arctic air tomorrow night and Monday, uh, strong winds and, uh, temperatures only in the twenties on Monday despite a lot of sunshine, but it's gonna feel like low teens or single-digits. Tuesday, without the wind, it won't feel as harsh, clouds, a little bit of sun, and temperatures recover into the mid-thirties. We have thirty-six and a cloudy sky, with a south wind at seven. Repeating the current temperature thirty-six going down to thirty-five in midtown.

A kind of a damp day out there today, well, periods of rain will continue through the evening hours, some of that rain may be heavy for the next few hours, we'll have a high of forty-four degrees. Winds will increase tonight, it becomes much colder with clearing skies, falling back to nineteen. Watch for some slippery patches if you're out driving around late tonight. For tomorrow, brittle and cold wind with sunshine, we'll have a high of twenty-eight, but the RealFeel temperature is only in the low teens and single digits. Not quite as harsh for Tuesday with times of clouds and sunshine, high near forty. And now Wednesday, cloudy and windy with a chance of rain, a high of forty-six. Currently thirty-five degrees in White

Plains, thirty-four in Bridgeport, in Central Park thirty-eight degrees, relative humidity one hundred percent, and the wind out of the northeast at six miles per hour. Repeating the current temperature thirty-eight heading up to forty-four in midtown.

We are awaiting some bitterly cold air that will be arriving in the tri-state area in a matter of hours, the current radar showing a few light snow showers, flurries, really, uh, for instance right now, Sommerville, New Jersey getting those flurries, while Teterborough Airport is getting a few sprinkles. The arctic front moves through, and even though it's thirty-nine now, we'll be plunging all the way to twenty-two later this morning. Later today temperatures stay in the twenties, and it'll feel like it's in the low teens when you factor in the wind so, uh, not, uh, good stuff, more like early January rather than early March. It'll be eighteen on this Monday night, we'll recover to a high of about forty Tuesday. Just when it looks like things are gonna be better, and it'll be around fifty or so Wednesday, we could see some rain in the afternoon. Thirty-nine in midtown right now, relative humidity fifty-seven percent, wind west ten miles per hour, gusting to twenty. Fair, thirty-nine, we're heading down to twenty-two.

This is, uh, a little silly here with temperatures around twenty-one degrees. We should actually be in the mid-forties at this time of the year, so some twenty-six, twenty-six degrees below normal this afternoon and, uh, tonight, uh, we're gonna need several logs on the fire too. Fifteen in midtown, ten in a lot of the suburbs. Clear skies, uh, the better part of the night, but it is going to be clouding up before morning. Uh, tomorrow, clouds, some breaks of sun, but, uh, we'll finally get the air mass to moderate a little bit, thirty-seven in the afternoon. Uh, tomorrow night it doesn't drop hardly at all, could even see a bit of rain late tomorrow night. Wednesday, intermittent rain, but at least it's a little bit milder too, with temperatures getting up to around fifty in the afternoon. Thursday, though, it's, uh, windy and turning colder once again, clouds breaking for some sun, high of thirty-six, and then Friday we'll bounce into the mid-forties, as it clouds up once again. Twenty-one and sunny, the RealFeel reading is nine on a northwest wind, ten to twenty miles an hour. Repeating the current temperature twenty-one going down to fifteen in midtown.

It is cold again this morning, although not as bitter as yesterday, and the leading edge of warmer air, or a warm front, is pushing through the area today, uh, that's producing cloud cover now. There are even a few light flurries around, most of them are north of the city,

Sussex, Passaic, northern Bergen counties in New Jersey, and then Orange, Rockland, northern Rockland, Westchester, and Putnam counties. Uh, there, uh, it'll be a couple of light flurries, but there'll also be some sun as we go through the mid-day and afternoon, and it will get milder up into the thirties. The temperature won't drop much tonight. We will have drizzle, rain, and fog tomorrow with a high forty-five to fifty. When the rain begins late tonight, it still could be cold enough north and west for there to be a little freezing rain and then, uh, it clears on Thursday, uh, chilly again with a high in the thirties. Right now it's twenty-one, mostly cloudy in Central Park, temperature today going up to thirty-seven.

Well, yes and, uh, we should plan on most of that rain occurring between the hours of, uh, five o'clock on this Wednesday morning and around noontime, so it will have an impact on the morning rush hour and, uh, even more so, we're concerned about some of that rain freezing on some surfaces north and west of the city. Many counties in northern New Jersey, Rockland and Orange counties, Westchester, northern Westchester, New York, are under winter weather advisories for that reason. Keep in mind, even though it's thirty-nine in midtown right now, and there's been no change within the past couple of hours, many suburbs near thirty. So we've got that to contend with. But everybody'll getting . . . it will be getting milder on Wednesday afternoon when the rain stops, highs will be close to fifty degrees. We'll turn drier on Wednesday night and Thursday but also colder, Wednesday night, the low twenty-nine, Thursday's high in the mid-thirties, Friday forty-three, and rain may return, especially late in the day or at night. Mostly cloudy, thirty-nine in midtown, relative humidity seventy-six percent, the air is calm. It's mostly cloudy and thirty-nine, heading down to thirty-four.

Well, we're looking at, uh, just a stray shower this evening, but otherwise mild, uh, here early this evening. It will be turning, uh, chillier during the night behind a cold front, with temperatures getting down around the freezing mark by daybreak. Uh, for tomorrow it's a cloudy, brisk, colder day and we've got a storm, uh, developing over Arkansas, with some rain breaking out that's going to be spreading northeast. Word now is that there's some wet snow starting around daybreak, uh, probably ending during the afternoon hours. Right now, looks like a one to three inch, uh, snowfall, uh, with the roads wet and slushy, as temperatures just kind of hover near freezing. It'll clear out tomorrow night, and then it's a stretch of some nice weather Friday, through the weekend, uh, at least partly sunny skies, and temperatures getting back into the forties. Right now we have fifty-one, mostly cloudy skies, and a southwest wind at twelve. Repeating the current temperature fifty-one, going down to thirty-two in midtown.

Well, in the wake of our, uh, generally three to six inch snowstorm we had earlier, uh, skies are going to be clearing out. Now, the rest of the night, uh, high pressure, which stretches from Michigan all the way down to the Mississippi Valley, is going to be sliding eastward and giving us very cold conditions overnight. The wind will settle down, that'll help because right now it feels like it's down in the single digits, temperatures are going to drop eighteen in midtown, ten in some of the suburbs. Underneath the center of this high, not a bad day coming up tomorrow, sure it's chilly but, uh, lots of sunshine and lighter winds, the high of thirty-four. And then we're gonna warm it up as the high moves offshore this weekend, Saturday partly sunny and forty-nine, Sunday fifty-one degrees ahead of the next front, uh, it'll be a windy day on Sunday, uh, maybe a shower early on. Right now we have mostly cloudy skies, twenty-four degrees and a north wind, fifteen to twenty-five miles an hour. Repeating the current temperature twenty-four going down to eighteen in midtown.

We're looking at a, uh, nice, uh, weekend weather-wise. Tonight partly cloudy skies, temperatures in the upper-twenties in the city, low twenties in many of the suburbs. Uh, but milder air is going to be on the move here for the next couple of days. We'll see afternoon temperatures in the upper-forties, uh, both days, uh, featuring a little bit of sunshine and breezy tomorrow, uh, tomorrow night, actually late tomorrow night or first thing Sunday morning, we could see a shower or two, as a front moves through, uh, but, uh, with that front approaching, tomorrow night's gonna be quite mild, a low of forty degrees. And then Sunday, uh, becoming windy behind the front, clouds, some sunshine, and high of forty-nine. Colder air does come in then to start the new week, um, Monday mostly sunny, brisk, and a high of thirty-four. Clouding up Tuesday, we may even see a little snow, especially Tuesday afternoon, a high of thirty-six. We have thirty degrees and mostly cloudy sky in Central Park, a southwest breeze at seven. Repeating the current temperature, thirty going down to twenty-eight in midtown.

Well, temperatures aren't going to be falling too much this evening ahead of a cold front, in fact they may rise a little bit as we head through the overnight hours. Uh, we're gonna see those clouds start to increase, low near forty degrees, maybe a shower or two by dawn and early tomorrow, with a cold front moving on through. In the wake of that front, it turns windy for tomorrow afternoon, some sunshine returning, high forty-nine degrees but, uh, temperatures should fall during the afternoon. Mainly clear, windy, and colder tomorrow night, low twenty-one. A cold, gusty wind continuing on Monday, sunny to partly cloudy, high thirty-four, partly sunny on Tuesday, the high thirty-eight. We're at forty-two right now, mostly cloudy in Central Park, humidity fifty-seven percent, the wind southeast at thirteen miles an hour, and repeating the current temperature forty-two, going down to forty in midtown.

Temperature continues to drop like a stone here. We're down into the middle-twenties now, easily going to be getting into the teens in many locations, maybe around twenty in midtown, enough wind to make it feel like it's down into the single digits overnight. Right now the RealFeel reading eleven and, uh, we will see, uh, a cold wind continue right on through the day tomorrow, lots of sunshine. We'll struggle to get back near the freezing mark, and then drop back into the teens again tomorrow night. Tuesday, as this, uh, arctic high gets off the East Coast, we'll start a moderating trend, get back to forty in the afternoon with sunshine. Wednesday, a windy day once again, as another front moves through but, uh, otherwise, clouds and sunshine, expecting temperatures in the mid-forties. Currently twenty-seven in Newark, twenty-six degrees and, uh, clear skies in Central Park, we have a northwest wind still, fifteen to twenty-five miles an hour. Repeating the current temperature twenty-six, going down to twenty in midtown.

This is going to be the coldest day of the week, and tonight a very cold night, but after that the temperature trend will be upward, modestly, but upward nevertheless. Today, uh, only in the twenties to near thirty, despite plenty of sunshine, and, um, the wind, uh, certainly this morning making it feel a lot colder than that, that RealFeel temperature even, uh, near zero at times. Tomorrow, uh, and Wednesday will be partly sunny and it will get milder. Tomorrow, temperatures take a run up toward forty, on Wednesday they'll run into the forties, and may even take a run toward fifty. Next chance of any rain, or any rain and snow comes along about Thursday. Right now it's twenty-two and sunny in Central Park, humidity forty-three percent, wind from the northwest at ten, that makes the RealFeel temperature sixteen. Repeating the current temperature twenty-two, going up to twenty-nine today.

Well, uh, I guess, uh, this is a tranquil weather pattern from the standpoint that we're not talking about any major storms this week, uh, but it's still cold, bottom line, twenty-five and clear in midtown, we're heading down to twenty overnight in many suburbs. We'll be in the teens early tomorrow morning, seems like about the, uh, hundredth morning, uh, since November that we've been in the twenties or lower. Well, uh, tomorrow somewhat of an improvement after a high of just twenty-nine today, with a partly sunny sky, high will be close to forty. Tomorrow night, not as cold as tonight, lows only in the mid-thirties, and with a south-west wind. Wednesday, we'll, uh, get temperatures up to a very mild fifty-two. Thursday, though, it looks colder again, a weak weather system may produce some rain or wet snow Thursday afternoon or night, and then Friday clouds break and we'll, uh, settle into readings in the mid-forties, not too far from the seasonal average for this time of year. Clear and twen-ty-five right now, relative humidity thirty-seven percent, northwest winds six miles per hour. It is clear and twenty-five, we're heading down to twenty.

Well, we've got some nice weather coming up for tomorrow on a southwesterly flow ahead of an approaching cold front. Uh, we'll have a milder afternoon with temperatures climbing into the fifties, uh, clouds and some sunshine, but once that front goes through, we're back down into the thirties later tomorrow night and Thursday. And in addition to the chillier air, we're also going to have to deal with a system coming all the way from the Pacific Northwest, uh, which is likely to generate, uh, a cold rain, perhaps even some wet snow on Thursday with, like I said, temperatures, uh, in the mid-and-upper-thirties. Once that gets off-shore, we will be clearing out, uh, with, uh, temperatures back into the forties on Friday. And it looks like some nice weather for the upcoming weekend, milder once again, mostly sunny Saturday and fifty-two. Central Park reporting thirty-six degrees under a partly cloudy sky, we have a southwest wind at eight. Repeating the current temperature thirty-six going down to thirty-four in midtown.

Well, we have a cold front, uh, which is on our doorstep. This'll be slipping through here this evening, uh, with, uh, little more, uh, than a sprinkle. Uh, our radar showing just some light echoes, uh, near the city and just to our north, a lot of this is probably not even reach-ing the ground, uh, otherwise mostly cloudy tonight, a low of thirty-six. Uh, tomorrow is a much chillier day, we're looking at temperatures staying in the upper-thirties, uh, there is a wave of low pressure, which is gonna run along this boundary. We expect to see some rain develop during the morning hours, that'll, uh, change over to wet snow from north to south, as we go through the day and could, uh, amount to, uh, a slushy coating to an inch on the non-paved surfaces as, uh, temperatures will be staying above freezing. It's going to have a hard time sticking to roadways, and the best chance of that, obviously, higher elevations across northern New Jersey and into, uh, southeastern New York state, uh, actually in that region there could be an inch or two. Uh, tomorrow night we'll clear out, it does get cold, the low of twenty-six, but then some nice weather Friday through the weekend. Friday mostly sunny and forty-two, and then we'll jump into the fifties with sunshine Saturday and Sunday. Forty-nine and cloudy at the moment, a southwest wind at eight. Repeating the current temperature forty-one going down to thirty-six in midtown.

We do have some rain and snow on the way today, but still not yet for a couple of hours, uh, and so, uh, we'll be OK, uh, getting through the rest of the morning rush hour. Then it'll begin to rain, uh, the rain will change fairly quickly to snow late this morning in the northern and western suburbs, continue this afternoon, north and west of Interstate 287. In the usual spots there can be an inch, or two, or maybe three, that accumulates. In the city, rain could mix with some sleet or some wet snow, but the temperature will be above freezing and the, uh, sleet and snow will melt when it hits the ground. We're not anticipating any accumulation. Clearing tonight, mostly sunny tomorrow, high around forty, at least partly sunny Saturday with a high near fifty, into the fifties Sunday with increasing clouds. Right now forty-two and cloudy in Central Park, temperature today going down slowly to thirty-four.

The weekend's going to get milder, so hang in there. We'll get through today, uh, it will be a partly to mostly sunny day, but the high temperature only in the upper-thirties, and fair and cold tonight, low in the twenties, probably the teens in the northern suburbs. Tomorrow it will be partly sunny, and it will get milder, up to forty-eight. The trend toward milder weather continues Sunday, with a high in the low fifties, although Sunday there will be an increase in cloudiness, and on Sunday, there will also be a breeze off the water so, uh, from the south, which means the Rockaways, uh, the south shore of Long Island, the Five Towns, that area, will tend to be cooler, probably staying in the forties, then some rain Sunday night and Monday. Twenty-two and partly cloudy now in Central Park, temperature today going up to thirty-eight.

Well, uh, certainly the weather will be treating us a lot more kindly over the next few days. I mean, sure, we're going to encounter some cloud cover, and even a bit of rain early Monday perhaps and, uh, more rain can occur Wednesday and Thursday, but there will be long stretches of time that will be dry, and no arctic air is coming, that's the bottom line. Eh, you may remember two out of the last three Sunday nights and Mondays, we had a visit from arctic air. Not this time around. Temperatures will be near forty later on this Sunday morning. Today we're expecting a high in the mid-fifties in midtown, cooler on Long Island, warmer in the western suburbs. It's always that way this time of year, whenever you get a warm-up. Now, uh, as I said, a bit of rain possible Monday, but still a high will be about fifty-four, and we'll be near fifty Tuesday and Wednesday. Right now in midtown forty-eight and fair, and that relative humidity fifty-eight percent, the wind variable seven miles per hour. Repeating the current temperature forty-eight, heading down to forty.

Well, we will see some clouds increasing through the evening. We'll actually turn out mostly cloudy tonight, and we do expect to see some patches of fog and drizzle, especially after midnight, low forty-six. Tomorrow, cloudy in the morning where there is fog and drizzle still around, then clouds may break for some afternoon sunshine, bringing in another mild afternoon with a high around sixty. Patches of clouds tomorrow night, low forty-eight degrees. Clouds and some sun on Tuesday with a high of fifty-seven, partly sunny and noticeably cooler Wednesday, high forty-eight degrees. Cloudy on Thursday with a chance for rain and drizzle, Thursday's high again, around forty-eight degrees. Sixty right now in midtown, the relative humidity is sixty-one percent, winds light and variable. Repeating the current temperature, sixty going down to forty-six in midtown.

Well, for too long the air felt like it was coming from Greenland, but for today it's coming from Shamrock, Texas, Cloverleaf, and also Greenville, South Carolina. It'll be mild, going to sixty-four, partly cloudy tonight, low forty-eight. Tomorrow partly sunny, high fifty-seven, chillier Wednesday, with clouds and sun, high forty-six, it's likely to rain on Thursday. Currently in midtown forty-nine degrees, relative humidity eighty-three percent, wind northeast three miles per hour, forty-nine heading for sixty-four.

There's going to be some sunshine today. The temperature will get up to sixty, uh, interior sections could get into the low sixties, maybe not like seventy, uh, like we got yesterday, but still, pretty comfortable. Then tonight will be partly cloudy, it'll chill down into the thirties. A cooler day tomorrow, with the wind off the water, and a mix of clouds and sun, high tomorrow forty-four. Clouding up, followed by some rain Thursday, especially late Thursday, Thursday night and into Friday, Friday night, with Friday's high back into the fifties. Right now it's fifty-six and partly cloudy, or partly sunny in Central Park, temperature today going up to fifty-nine.

SPRING

Oh, we are looking at, uh, weather, uh, across, uh, Iraq obviously here for the next several days, uh, we have, uh, actually some good, good weather is expected. They did have a sandstorm here earlier, uh, over the last twelve to twenty-four hours those winds have subsided and will actually continue to subside. Uh, there will be enough of a wind across the southern portion of the country that still may cause some blowing sand tomorrow. Otherwise we're looking at clear to partly cloudy skies tonight and tomorrow, uh, the weekend, uh, it is good weather, and then we could have a storm, uh, generating some strong winds, uh, for Sunday night and Monday, uh, even the possibility of a little rain in Baghdad. Uh, currently we have, uh, uh, increasing cloudiness, uh, forecast locally tonight, uh, it's gonna be brisk and chilly, temperatures getting down into the middle-thirties, and then some, uh, intermittent rain is expected tomorrow and tomorrow night. It'll become steadier and heavier late in the day and, uh, actually a pretty good soaking tomorrow night. Uh, temperatures getting into the mid-forties tomorrow, and then staying in the forties tomorrow night. Friday it's a breezy and warmer day but, uh, still a few more showers maybe even a thunderstorm, the high of sixty degrees. Currently we have sunshine and forty-four with an east wind of ten. Repeating the current temperature forty-four, going up to forty-six in midtown.

We still have clouds, we still have some fog outside of the city this morning but, uh, during the afternoon the sky can brighten, the sun can peek on through, temperatures get on up into the sixties. A couple of showers and maybe a thunderstorm this evening, and then the weekend to follow looks pretty good, at least partly sunny. It'll be breezy tomorrow, the high about sixty and in the, uh, fifties for a high on Sunday. As for Middle East weather, it continues to be favorable for military operations, and that'll remain the case through Sunday, but Monday and Tuesday, there may be another episode of strong winds, poor visibilities, and, uh, even some sandstorms. Right now fifty-seven and cloudy in Central Park, temperature today going up to sixty-two.

Well, sunshine will be mixing with clouds as we go through the day today. It is going to be on the mild side again this afternoon, the high up to sixty-four degrees in midtown today. Tonight, we're partly cloudy, dropping back to a low of forty-two. We're gonna stay dry tomorrow and Monday as well. Partly to mostly sunny skies, highs in the mid-to-upper-fifties, and then back to sixty-four for a high on Tuesday, with increasing clouds. No chance of rain in sight until we get to the day Wednesday. Dry weather in Baghdad for the rest of the weekend as well, partly cloudy skies Saturday night, and also some sunshine across Baghdad on Sunday. Right now it's fifty-four degrees and sunny in Central Park, we're going up to sixty-four in midtown today.

With sunshine, the temperature's headed on up to sixty-one for the high this afternoon, partly to mostly cloudy tonight the . . . or clear to partly cloudy tonight, I should say, the low forty-six in midtown, forty in many suburbs. Tomorrow another mild day, going towards sixty-four with sunshine, then a cold front will arrive Wednesday with a couple of showers, high sixty. Rain could follow Wednesday night and Thursday morning if that front stalls and a low pressure area forms along it. Afterwards, Thursday afternoon, high fifty-four with some sunshine. In Iraq, the winds are likely to be picking up in the next twenty-four hours, raising more sand and dust into the atmosphere, and that's going to be a problem through Wednesday. Things should settle down after that, after the current storm from the Mediterranean moves past. Currently, the winds are light and variable, the relative humidity forty-six percent, fifty-five in midtown heading for sixty-one.

A nice evening, clear to partly cloudy skies overnight. We'll be in the mid-forties come daybreak, uh, tomorrow another mild day but, uh, clouds and, uh, limited sun, a couple of showers around associated with a cold front which will be moving through, especially in the afternoon and evening. Clears out later tomorrow night, and Thursday and Friday lots of sunshine and only, uh, a bit cooler, fifty-four Thursday, fifty-eight Friday. The battlefield forecast, uh, the weather is nasty over there right now. Strong winds accompanying a powerful cold front, uh, really kicking up the sand and making for poor visibility. Uh, that wind speed will gradually come down over the next twenty-four hours, but it'll still be causing some problems.

Rain, in mountains, snow in northern Iraq on Wednesday, a couple of showers still down in Baghdad, uh, then better weather Thursday, right on through the weekend. Back home we have fifty-seven in Caldwell, fifty-three and sunshine in Central Park, the southeast wind at eleven. Repeating the current temperature fifty-three going down to forty-seven in midtown.

Well, not much on the radar, literally, just one shower up over northern Bergen County, and also over northeastern Morris County. And as they move off to the northeast, the balance of this afternoon is on the dry side, so you really don't need the umbrella for the most part here, sixty-eight degrees for the afternoon high. What we'll see, in terms of showers, will be for the evening rush hour, through the remainder of this evening, but already by daybreak the clouds are parting company in the wake of our most recent cool front. We're in at forty degrees, and, yeah, we're gonna cool it, now, that's what a front does. Despite the sun back there'll be a breeze tomorrow, high fifty-six. Sunshine, patchy clouds Friday with a high of fifty-eight degrees. As for our battlefield forecast, one or two showers left over the northern two-thirds of, uh, Iraq during the course of this evening, but better weather ahead later tonight and over the next couple of days, as the wind dies down. Around here, not much wind, it's seventy in Morristown, sixty-six Belmar, sixty-four and partly sunny in Central Park going to sixty-eight in midtown.

We'll look for sunshine to be with us, uh, all day today, and temperatures will respond and get up to about the sixty degree mark, and then it'll be partly cloudy tonight, low forty-four. Increasing clouds tomorrow, a little cooler, thanks to a breeze coming in off the water, high tomorrow fifty-six. Rain at times Saturday, Saturday night, ending Sunday morning, but brisk and, uh, pretty cool the rest of the day Sunday, with the temperature not getting much at all above fifty. Weather conditions in Iraq, uh, and Kuwait have improved, ur, improved considerably over the last twenty-four hours. Skies are clear, visibilities are much better, winds are much, much lighter, and it does not look like weather is going to be, uh, any kind of a major player for at least the next few days. Around these parts, it's forty-five and sunny in Central Park, temperature today going up to sixty.

Sunshine still with us and temperature still climbing, and it should get to sixty, and even into the sixties today. It'll be coolest on the south shore of Long Island and the Connecticut coast with a southerly breeze coming in off the water. Then it clouds up tonight, could start to drizzle. We get drizzle and rain at times tomorrow, especially tomorrow night on into Sunday morning, could be some heavy rain and maybe a thunderstorm. The rain, um, er, probably at least the steady rain, ends Sunday morning, but there still may be some rain showers around Sunday afternoon, and it will be noticeably colder with temperatures no higher than the forties. Right now, though, uh, it is fifty-six degrees and sunny in Central Park, and the temperature today going up to, uh, about sixty.

Brisk and cold today, clouds and sunshine. We're going to have a high temperature near forty-two degrees and, for the Mets home opener, the RealFeel temperature upper-twenties and low thirties, so definitely a bundle-up time, but a dry afternoon. Partly to mostly cloudy tonight, low thirty in midtown, twenty-four in outlying areas. Tomorrow turns out cloudy, and as a warm front approaches, we'll have some rain in the afternoon, could start as a little wet snow, but the temperature by end of the day, forty-four northern suburbs, fifty in central Jersey, well up in the forties in the city. Wednesday variable cloudiness, with a shower possible, high fifty, then into the fifties with a few showers on Thursday. Meanwhile on the battlefield, sunshine, seventies today, but nineties by the end of the week in many areas. Currently in midtown thirty-two degrees, relative humidity fifty-one percent, wind west northwest at twelve, thirty-two heading for forty-two.

Clouds thickening over the next couple of hours, then we expect some rain during the midday and early afternoon hours, could be some wet snow mixed in the beginning but it won't stick. High today forty-two, tonight's low forty. Tomorrow, some clouds and sun, perhaps a shower, high fifty-four. Then we'll be close to the boundary between cool air and warm air on Thursday and Friday. We're calling Thursday, clouds and sunshine, maybe a shower, high fifty-nine, then Friday partly sunny and warmer, high sixty-eight degrees, with a thunderstorm possibility in the afternoon. On the battlefield, temperatures in the eighties in the afternoon hours through midweek, getting closer to one hundred as we close out the week. Currently in midtown thirty-three degrees, relative humidity forty-nine percent, wind north at five miles per hour, thirty-three heading for forty-two.

Uh, it looks like the next couple of days we're gonna be close to a boundary between warm air, with temperatures in the seventies from Philadelphia southward, however, in upstate New York it probably stays in the thirties and forties, hopefully we get into the fifties today and tomorrow with a few breaks of sunshine. Central New Jersey and on, uh, inland, it can get into the sixties. It can always sprinkle or shower but, uh, at least through tomorrow we're not looking for much in the way of rain. Friday, rather cloudy, cool, high in the fifties, uh, chance of showers, maybe a late day thunderstorm. And then pretty cool on Saturday, may not get above fifty with some rain likely. Sunday partly sunny, but chilly, with a high of forty-eight. Right now it is forty-five and mostly cloudy in Central Park, temperature today going up to fifty-four.

A mostly cloudy, cool day coming up today, the temperature will get to about fifty, or maybe or maybe the low fifties, and that's about it, drops back to about forty with some clouds and patchy fog and drizzle tonight. Then it'll start to rain tomorrow, probably late in the day, we'll have rain tomorrow night on into the day on Saturday, with a high Saturday into the fifties. No, uh, genuine prospects for sunshine until Sunday, but even then it'll be chilly, a high around fifty. Uh, battlefield weather is sunny and hot in, uh, Baghdad, the temperature into the low nineties at this moment, and it'll be middle-to-upper-nineties tomorrow, and over the weekend with one hundred degrees plus, in the southern and eastern deserts. Some gusty winds over the weekend could cause isolated pockets of, uh, blowing sand and reduced visibilities, but nothing near as widespread as last week. Right now it's forty-four and mostly cloudy in Central Park, temperature today going up to about fifty.

It's going to be overcast, drizzly, with some fog today. We'll have drizzle, rain, and fog tonight and tomorrow, uh, temperature today not going to go up much, it may even drop a couple of degrees, and the lows tonight will be near thirty in the northern and western suburbs, and that means there can be some freezing rain, as well as just rain, high temperatures tomorrow forty-five to fifty, Sunday mostly sunny with a high around fifty. The, uh, battlefield forecast, the heat will peak Saturday, with highs in Baghdad near one hundred, then not as hot Sunday and Monday, but windy at times. Those gusty winds will pick up some sand and dust, and cause areas of reduced visibility. Right now it is forty-one and cloudy in Central Park and our temperature today going up only to forty-three.

Oh, just a damp and chilly day underway. There will be some occasional light rain and drizzle, some areas of fog, and even a rumble or two of thunder, we'll have a high of just forty-four degrees, and then windy and cold, with clearing skies tonight, low thirty-six. A sunny but windy and chilly day, with a high around fifty degrees. Monday, cloudy, windy, and cold with some snow, sleet, and rain, and we're probably going to be talking accumulations north and west of the city, Monday's high just forty degrees, though. Cloudy, with a chance for lingering rain Tuesday, especially during the morning, with a high around fifty, and partly sunny Wednesday, with a high around near fifty degrees. Battlefield forecast is as follows, we do have a partly cloudy sky with gusty winds over Saturday night, and a mix of clouds and sun, with blowing sand and dust on Sunday. It's thirty-seven degrees right now, heading up to forty-four in midtown.

We are going to have increasing and thickening clouds tonight, and, uh, temperatures will, for the most part, be between twenty-five and thirty-two at daybreak on Monday. Then get ready for the snow. It will tend to mix with some sleet and freezing rain in some locations, uh, but we're looking at a significant accumulation, especially for this time of year, uh, most places will get between four and eight inches. We've got the winter storm warnings in effect for Monday and early Monday night. It should wind down Monday night as a few flurries and some drizzle. Still, it's going to be tough getting around tomorrow, so allow yourself some extra time. The high tomorrow in the mid-thirties, Monday night's low about thirty degrees, and it's going to be cloudy on Tuesday, Wednesday, and Thursday and on the cool side. The battlefield forecast, Baghdad tomorrow, could be a rain or, uh, thunderstorm, uh, shower. Temperatures will be in the upper-eighties. It'll be hotter Tuesday. Back home, forty-one in midtown right now, clear, relative humidity forty-four percent, the wind northeast seven miles per hour. Clear and forty-one heading down to thirty-two.

It's getting closer and closer now. It is now snowing now in Hunterdon and Somerset counties, parts of southern Morris and Union counties as well, and the snow is spreading eastward. It will spread across the metropolitan area within the next hour to two hours, and then we look for heavy snow this afternoon, and on into this evening, with an average accumulation across the metropolitan area of four to eight inches. Keep in mind during the day today, during the daylight hours, temperatures high enough so that a lot of the snow is going to melt, at least initially, on city streets and highways and parkways, but they can get slushy and slippery in spots for sure, uh, there can even be, uh, a few extra inches in the hilly areas north and west of Interstate 287, but an average, we think, of four to six or eight inches across most of the tri-state area. Right now it's thirty-six and cloudy in Central Park, temperature today going down to thirty-two.

Well, a cloudy day today, uh, there's been a little drizzle, there's been a little freezing drizzle, there'll continue to be a little drizzle at times, uh, during the day today, with a high of thirty-six. We look for some rain, eh, at times tonight and tomorrow, low tonight thirty-four, and the high tomorrow forty. It's cloudy Thursday, there's still the chance for some rain, a high in the forties. And then we may have a major storm, uh, even a nor'easter, come up the eastern seaboard Friday, Friday night, into Saturday morning. Odds favor rain, coastal areas, and maybe some gusty winds as well, high tides and all of that, clearing beginning later on Saturday. Right now it's thirty-one and cloudy in Central Park, temperature today going up to thirty-six.

We've got rain all across the metropolitan area now, there's been a little bit of sleet that's bounced around but this is, uh, mostly just a cold, wet, nasty rain and it'll rain pretty steadily into the middle part of the afternoon with, uh, a high of thirty-eight. Clouds tonight, low thirty-four. Variable cloudiness tomorrow, perhaps a few brighter intervals, and, uh, if we, uh, get even a little bit of sun, the temperature tomorrow will get into the forties. Clouds, rain and wind back for Friday, in fact, could be pretty stormy, Friday afternoon and Friday night, with winds gusting, perhaps to forty miles an hour. Clearing begins Saturday afternoon, and Sunday looks mostly sunny and pleasant with a high near sixty. Right now it's thirty-five and cloudy in Central Park, temperature today going up to thirty-eight.

Well, it will be a cool and breezy day today, but no rain, and although there'll be a lot of clouds, uh, the sun will peek out from time to time, in place to place, and that gets temperatures into the forties for the first time all week long. Tomorrow, though, a rainy windy day, uh, windy, chilly with temperatures in the low to middle-forties, and some of the rain, tomorrow, tomorrow night, will be heavy enough to cause street and highway flooding. It clears on Saturday and Sunday looks good, mostly sunny and the high fifty-six to sixty. Iraqi weather has cooled down, it'll be dry through the weekend, relatively comfortable, sixties in the northern part of the country and, uh, no higher than the eighties in Baghdad. Right now in Central Park, forty degrees and cloudy, the high today forty-eight.

Well, it's not very nice outside, and it's not going to get a whole lot, uh, in fact, probably not going to get any better, as we go through the day. We're going to have rain intermittent today and tonight, and into tomorrow morning, some of the rain will be heavy, eh, other times, the rain can stop completely. And there will also continue to be a gusty wind, that wind gusting frequently to thirty miles per hour, and occasionally to between thirty and forty miles per hour. The temperature not much above forty, so not only is it wet, but it's kind of nasty and cold. Clearing tomorrow afternoon, though, and with the sun coming out, temperatures will jump into the fifties, and then Sunday should be mostly sunny, with a high around sixty. But right now, it's forty and raining in Central Park, and that wind out of the northeast, gusting to twenty-nine miles per hour. Repeating the current temperature forty, going up to forty-four today.

It looks like the rain has ended in New York City, it should be ending across Long Island in the next couple of hours. Clouds will break for sunshine, from west to east, across the area we'll have a high of sixty. Mostly clear, brisk, cold tonight, low falling back to about forty-two. It'll be mostly sunny tomorrow, the high of fifty-eight, partial sunshine. Nice day for your Monday, high sixty-four. Sunshine, breezy, turning much warmer for Tuesday, with the high of seventy-three degrees. Currently fifty-four degrees in Bridgeport, some rain out in Islip, fifty-one, in Central Park, fifty-seven degrees, relative humidity seventy-four percent, wind out the north, northwest at ten miles per hour. Repeating the current temperature fifty-seven going up to sixty in midtown.

Well, the region will be basting in plenty of sunshine that'll be overhead via the area of high pressure that moved in over the last twelve to twenty-four hours, a breezy and nice afternoon with the high of fifty-eight degrees. Clear and cool tonight, low forty midtown, thirty-four in the suburbs. And we'll see more in the way of sunshine, as we head through the middle part of the week, temperatures actually moderating, as we head through the day on Monday and Tuesday. Breezy Monday, high sixty-four, windy Tuesday, with a high of seventy-six degrees, sunshine, patchy clouds, breezy and warm, a high again of seventy-six. Forty-six degrees and sunny in Central Park, humidity fifty-eight percent, wind north at three miles per hour. Repeating the current temperature forty-six, we're headed up to fifty-eight in midtown.

Ah, still a dazzling day out there with bright sunshine, temperatures are, uh, almost to fifty degrees right now, and we expect them to top out into the sixties today. It will be a gentle sea breeze that keeps shore points cooler, but then, uh, tonight will be, uh, fair and relatively mild, with a low about fifty and tomorrow, a gusty southwest wind combines with sunshine and temperatures tomorrow will be off to the races, eighty or above inland areas, probably at least seventy-eight or eighty in midtown, cooler on the south shore of Long Island and the Connecticut coast, where the breeze comes in off the water. Still warm Wednesday, but could be a late day thunderstorm, and then it will be noticeably cooler Thursday and Friday, both of those days, eh, probably clouds, and the chance of rain and the high temperatures, not much above fifty. Right now, though, forty-eight and bright and sunny in Central Park, temperature today going up to sixty-four.

Well for today and tomorrow, it will seem like we have sprung right past spring and into summer, but by the end of the week, by Thursday and Friday, we will have fallen back toward winter. But today and tomorrow, if you're a warm weather fan, will be to your liking. Sunshine, patchy clouds, a gusty southwest wind, and in midtown as well as in adjacent New Jersey and the Hudson Valley, temperatures will climb to between eighty and eighty-five, while it stays closer to seventy on the south shore of Long Island and the Connecticut coast. Thursday, though, we turn things around. A cold front passes through Wednesday night that could produce a shower or a thunderstorm, and Thursday and Friday will be noticeably chillier with clouds, uh, some drizzle or rain, and temperatures no higher than the forties. Right now, though, we're already fifty-three and mostly sunny in Central Park, the temperature today going up to seventy-five.

We've got one more for you, but then quite a dramatic change tomorrow, but for the rest of the day today, sunshine, a few patchy high clouds, a gusty breeze out of the southwest, and high temperatures getting to between eighty and eighty-five in midtown, across most of New Jersey, and up the Hudson Valley. Long Island will be cooler, especially the south shore, maybe a shower tonight. And it will turn colder overnight, with a low near forty, and a dramatically colder day tomorrow, some forty degrees colder than today, with afternoon temperatures no higher than the forties. Remaining cloudy, chilly Friday, chance for some rain, clouds breaking for some sun Saturday, up to fifty-six, and Easter Sunday looks OK, partly sunny with a high of sixty-two. Right now, sixty-seven and sunshine in Central Park, temperature today going up to eighty-three.

Well, once again the radar showing some of the, er, showers right along the, uh, Essex, Union County line, just off to the north of Interstate 78, crossing, eh, 280, eh, once you get, eh, past, eh, West Orange, eh, Livingston, in through that corridor, as well as, eh, Bloomfield, Caldwell, so if you're in through this corridor, you've definitely got some wet weather to contend with as well as, uh, well, southern areas of Brooklyn down along the, um, er, well, down along the Belt Parkway. Quite honestly, once you get, eh, south of, eh, Linden Boulevard we have, uh, a couple of showers to contend with. We'll also get a little sun this afternoon, but, oh, that cold wind means business, with the high of forty-six degrees, and while it may drizzle tonight and tomorrow, well, most of the time it's just going to be cloudy, cold, thirty-six tonight, fifty tomorrow. Even Saturday's a damp start, but we should see a little late day sun with the high of fifty-eight, so at least it does turn somewhat milder. Right now, though, it's only thirty-nine Belmar, forty-three with the clouds Central Park, only going to forty-six this afternoon in midtown.

Uh, a cloudy, chilly, and brisk day, uh, temperature this afternoon will only be in the forties, the wind will still be gusting to about twenty miles an hour. There can be a bit of drizzle, there can be bit of rain, the same goes for tonight, and on into tomorrow morning. After that we do look for a slow improvement, the sky brightens tomorrow afternoon, the sun may come out, temperatures get into the fifties, and then Easter Sunday looks OK, mixed clouds and sun, the sunrise temperature about forty-five, the afternoon high on Sunday should be into the sixties. Right now, though, it's thirty-eight and cloudy in Central Park, humidity at ninety-two percent, wind from the east, gusting to twenty-one miles an hour. Repeating the current temperature thirty-eight, going up to forty-eight today.

Well, it's shaping up to be a pretty nice day across the tri-state area. So far lots of sunshine, uh, this morning, it looks like the sunshine will be sticking around through much of the day, and with that sunshine, temperatures up near sixty degrees in midtown for the afternoon. We stay dry tonight with clear to partly cloudy skies. Tomorrow's partly sunny as well, and the high goes back up to sixty in the afternoon, after a sunrise temperature tomorrow morning of forty-eight degrees. Clouds do return to the area Monday, and then Monday night into Tuesday, and we could see some rain, Monday's high sixty-four, Tuesday's high sixty. Currently sunny and forty-three degrees in Central Park, the humidity seventy percent, and the wind east at ten miles an hour. Again the current temperature forty-three, it'll go up to sixty in midtown.

Uh, mostly cloudy skies here for the remainder of the night, we'll see a few showers during the course of the night, maybe even a little fog developing, uh, with temperatures drifting down, uh, into the middle-forties. And then a mostly cloudy day Tuesday, as a front slowly works its way through the region, uh, this will generate a few showers, you may even hear a few rumbles of thunder, high temperature around fifty-nine. There's going to be a storm developing on that front, and that's why the wet weather for tomorrow, and that storm lifts up through New England, uh, later tomorrow night and Wednesday, and deepens, and the net result is that the wind'll pick up out of the northwest. It'll be cool, uh, we'll get some, uh, clearing, temperatures in the mid-forties tomorrow night, Wednesday around fifty-six, Thursday still kind of windy, but skies will be partly sunny, about sixty degrees, and then a nice day Friday. Currently in Central Park cloudy and forty-nine degrees, with a south wind at seven. Repeating the current temperature forty-nine going down to forty-six in midtown.

Indeed it is dreary and dull, damp, and dim. It's been this way since the day's dawn. Will it stay this way till its dreary and dull, dim, demise after dinner? We'll have to see but, if you live in eastern Nassau or Suffolk County, watch for some rain that's going to come ashore in about fifteen or twenty minutes, and sprinkle the area for about an hour. Rest of the area, not too much in the way of showers the next couple of hours, but there will be some more later today. Parts of the area can still have a thunderstorm, high fifty-nine. A leftover shower tomorrow tonight, low forty-six, then tomorrow becoming partly sunny, cool winds, gusty winds, temperatures won't get out of the fifties. Thursday looks like a nice day, still windy, high sixty-four, Friday sunshine, more tranquil, a high sixty-six. Currently forty-seven degrees, relative humidity one hundred percent, winds out of the northeast at eight miles per hour, forty-seven heading to fifty-nine.

We'll have a mixture of clouds and sunshine today, a gusty wind. It's going to be cool, temperature getting to about fifty-eight this afternoon, then clearing, windy, and chilly tonight, low forty-two in midtown, thirty-four in some suburbs. Now, as the high pressure area that's now in the Midwest moves toward us, tomorrow will be a sunny day with a gusty wind, but milder, high sixty-four late in the day, as the high pressure area moves offshore. Friday looks nice to start, followed by increasing cloudiness, high sixty-six, and a storm that's causing rain to spread across Kansas, Oklahoma, and Nebraska today, can reach us with rain Friday night into Saturday, Saturday's high fifty-six. Currently it's forty-six, relative humidity sixty-two percent, winds out of the west at ten, gusting to eighteen. Forty-six heading for, um, to fifty-eight.

Well, uh, the, uh, current radar filling in across the tri-state area, we're seeing, uh, fairly light rainfall right now, but we're anticipating that the intensity of the rain will be picking up very late tonight and tomorrow morning, uh, so a soggy Saturday definitely, uh, if you have some chores to do this weekend indoors, tomorrow would be the day to do them, and I think that Sunday, if you want to get outside, it'll be a much nicer day. But we're gonna be dealing with this storm system for the next twenty-four hours or so, the low overnight in midtown with the rain forty-eight, tomorrow's high only fifty-two, but as the rain comes to an end, probably tomorrow evening as some drizzle. You should see some late night clearing Sunday, it'll be a bit on the windy side, but with sunshine, highs will reach the mid-and-upper-sixties. Monday also will be about sixty-eight, our next shot at getting a shower, Tuesday. Cloudy, fifty-two in midtown, right now relative humidity eighty-nine percent, the wind variable, six miles per hour. Cloudy, fifty-two, we're heading down to forty-eight.

It's kind of a windy, wet, cool start to this weekend, in fact, uh, today looks like, eh, kind of a washout. Occasional rain, in fact, the rain can come down hard enough so that we could see a little bit of street and highway flooding, the high fifty-six. Tonight, drizzle in the evening then partial clearing, a low forty-eight. What a big improvement for Sunday with bright sunshine, a high of seventy degrees, sunny to partly cloudy, up to seventy-four on Monday. Uh, Tuesday it'll stay warm, we'll still go into the mid-seventies, but there is a chance for a shower. Right now we have forty-nine in White Plains, it's forty-seven in Bridgeport, cloudy and fifty in Central Park, with a humidity of one hundred percent, the winds east at nine. Repeating the current temperature fifty going up to fifty-six today.

Well it looks like our weather will be just beautiful for today, Monday looking nice, Tuesday even looks pretty nice, uh, even though a cold front will come through by then that could trigger a shower. But today, just sunshine and a high of sixty-eight, clear and comfortable tonight, fifty-four in midtown, forty-two in the suburbs. We'll go up to seventy-six with the sunshine tomorrow, cooler on the coast and on the Island, and on Tuesday, intervals of clouds and sun, as a cold front approaches the region, maybe a shower, the high seventy-four. Currently we have fifty degrees in Bridgeport and White Plains, partly sunny, fifty-two in Central Park, eighty-nine percent humidity, and northwest wind at nine. Fifty-two right now going up to sixty-eight.

We'll take it, huh? This is a beautiful day and, uh, actually, we've got nice weather for much of the, uh, coming week, uh, we've got, uh, mostly clear skies tonight, temperatures heading for the mid, upper-fifties, uh, even warmer tomorrow, eighty-two under a partly sunny sky. Uh, we will cool it down a little bit on Wednesday, there's going to be a front slipping through here tomorrow morning, uh, Wednesday will be in the upper-sixties, but that's still a nice day, lots of sunshine. Thursday, partly sunny and sixty-eight, Friday, low seventies. Uh, cloudy to partly sunny on Friday, and that's our first chance of seeing a shower or thunderstorm, as there will be a cold front moving through probably Friday evening. Right now sixty-six at JFK with a sea breeze, seventy-six in Central Park, sunny, and a south wind at twenty miles an hour. Repeating the current temperature seventy-six going down to fifty-eight in midtown.

Uh, we have, uh, it's, uh, a very small area of some light rain it's, uh, gonna be over very, very shortly, as a matter of fact, in the city and, uh, mmm, looking at definitely less than a tenth of an inch, uh, so it's just enough, uh, to hold the dust down, uh, the clouds leave, in part, for some sunshine once again for the late afternoon hours. Uh, temperatures obviously have cooled off here with the rain falling, and we will bounce back into, at least the lower seventies here, once, uh, uh, the clouds break up once again. Uh, the evening hours will be nice, and then tonight will be clear to partly cloudy, a low of fifty-two. Next couple of days, uh, some nice weather, lots of sunshine, sixty-eight tomorrow, partly sunny on Thursday with a high around seventy degrees. Uh, do expect to see some showers, maybe a thunderstorm in the, uh, Thursday night, Friday time period, that'll be the next, uh, front. Uh, could even be, uh, some steadier rain, uh, Friday night into Saturday, as a storm develops along that frontal boundary, then we'll start to clear out Saturday afternoon, Sunday should be nice. In Central Park reporting some light rain, and we've cooled off to sixty degrees, uh, still a northwest wind fifteen to twenty-five miles an hour. Repeating the current temperature sixty going up to seventy-nine in midtown.

Fine day today, cloudiness and some sunshine. There are a couple of showers, uh, twenty to thirty miles north of the city that'll bypass us, and we're going to have a very nice afternoon, uh, high temperature sixty-eight. Partly cloudy tonight, low fifty-two as the front that moved south of us yesterday, with a shower in the afternoon, moves back north as a warm front tomorrow. Can't rule out a shower, but overall, clouds and sunny breaks, the high seventy. Friday, clouds and some sun, a warm day high seventy-two, showers and thunderstorms possible, especially in the afternoon to tonight. Saturday looks like it'll start damp, but then turn partly sunny in the afternoon, high sixty-two. Currently, winds out of the north at four miles per hour, the relative humidity a low forty-three percent, fifty-five in midtown heading for sixty-eight.

Well, cloudiness today, there will be some showers around, they can occur just about any time, one batch of showers has gone by, but new ones are forming southwest. High sixty-six degrees, cooler on the south shore of Long Island and coastal Connecticut, partly to mostly cloudy and breezy tonight, low fifty-eight. Tomorrow, clouds wrap some sunny breaks, breezy and warm, but a pushing cold front can cause showers and thunderstorms just about any time, best chance is the afternoon and night. High seventy-two now. Assuming the front leaves, chance of morning rain, then clearing Saturday, front stalls, all bets are off on clearing. High Saturday sixty, Sunday looks to be sunny, high sixty-four. Currently in midtown, relative humidity ninety-two percent, the wind is out of the north at four miles per hour. It's fifty-four degrees heading for sixty-six.

It's a mild morning and it's going to be a warm day today, the temperatures likely to climb well into the seventies. Lots of sunshine for a while, then cloudiness during the course of the afternoon, there can be a thunderstorm. Any thunderstorm that develops can be strong and gusty, temperature today climbing well into the seventies. Then for tonight, clouds and a few showers and a thunderstorm, then tomorrow turning cooler, some sun by afternoon, low tonight fifty-two, high tomorrow sixty. Sunday looks like a sunny cool day, high sixty-four, Monday partly sunny, high sixty-four. Currently the winds out of the east at four miles per hour, the relative humidity eighty percent, sixty-two degrees, heading well up into the seventies this afternoon before cool air arrives.

Well, I suppose some folks might like it just a little warmer but, uh, it's still going to be very nice for early May today. We'll see sunshine, some clouds, a high of sixty-four. It'll mainly be clear and chilly tonight, we'll go down to thirty-eight in some of those colder suburbs, you know who you are, uh, down to about forty-eight in midtown. Sunshine followed by clouds tomorrow, still a cool breeze with a high of sixty-two, mostly cloudy with a cool breeze Tuesday, showers, maybe an afternoon thunderstorm, the high sixty to sixty-four. Warmer on Wednesday, but still a chance for a thunderstorm. Right now partly sunny, fifty-one in Central Park, it's forty-nine at Kennedy, and also at LaGuardia. It's fifty-one at Central Park, and it's going up to sixty-four.

We're gonna have increasing cloudiness today as that massive storm system from the middle of the country comes eastward, uh, we do not believe the risk of tornadic thunderstorms is, uh, very high here, but we're gonna get some rain starting either late this afternoon or early this evening. We'll have off and on rain tonight, and on into tomorrow, and it'll be kind of cool, with a breeze coming in off the water. Today it can get to sixty or a little bit above, but highs tomorrow not too far into the fifties. It'll get warmer Wednesday, clouds can break for some sun, could also be a shower or a thunderstorm, high Wednesday seventy-three, and then mostly cloudy on Thursday, high in the sixties. Right now it's fifty-four and partly sunny in Central Park, temperature today going up to sixty.

It's a gray, kind of a drizzly morning, and it's gonna stay that way all day, uh, there will be drizzle every now and then, there could be enough rain to form a puddle and to wet things down. The same goes for tonight, also areas of fog, and that fog could become pretty thick in places, uh, as we get into tonight and tomorrow morning. Temperatures today get into the fifties but, eh, probably not the sixties. Tomorrow we'll get milder, into the sixties, uh, then there's, uh, a period of rain, and maybe a thunderstorm tomorrow night into, into, eh, Thursday morning, followed by a dry period Thursday afternoon into Friday, but maybe more showers again later Friday. So, stringing a long period of dry weather, and certainly stringing a couple of sunny days in this weather pattern together is gonna be pretty tough. Right now it's forty-eight and cloudy in Central Park, the temperature today going up to fifty-eight.

It's cloudy and gray, but not much going on in terms of precipitation. We'll have a couple of showers around today, mostly this morning, but the vast majority of the time we'll just see clouds, high sixty-six. Partly to mostly cloudy tonight, low fifty-four, tomorrow a little brighter, clouds and sunny breaks, high about sixty-eight degrees, and Saturday should also be partly sunny, though a shower can't be ruled out, high sixty-eight. Showers a better bet for Sunday maybe a thunderstorm, high temperature sixty-eight on Mother's Day. Currently winds out of the east at seven miles per hour, the relative humidity ninety-six percent, fifty-eight degrees in midtown heading for sixty-six.

And what we have here tonight, is, uh, looks like, uh, dry weather from this point on. The light shower activity that, uh, was over the region is, uh, now moved offshore. Uh, partly to mostly cloudy skies, temperatures in the low to middle-fifties at daybreak, uh, tomorrow, a little bit of sunshine and a milder afternoon, upper-sixties to low seventies for a high. Maybe, uh, a shower, thunderstorm also in the afternoon or evening hours, but better chance for showers and th . . . uh, thunderstorms coming along later Sunday afternoon, Sunday night, that from a strong storm, which is, uh, still back in the Rockies right now. It'll be moving into Kansas tomorrow morning, and then up into the Great Lakes on Sunday, and, uh, sweeping, uh, a strong cold front over toward the East Coast, a high on Sunday around sixty-four. Currently we have sixty-three degrees, a cloudy sky, a southwest wind at eight. Repeating the current temperature sixty-three going down to fifty-four in midtown.

Mostly cloudy skies overnight, uh, temperatures in the mid-fifties come daybreak, and our Sunday will also be mostly cloudy, with a couple of rounds of showers and thunderstorms, mainly during the afternoon and early evening, as a strong cold front, uh, sweeps over to the eastern seaboard, a high temperature around sixty-five. Gusty winds and cool conditions both Monday and Tuesday, intervals of clouds and sunshine, just the possibility of a shower either day, sixty-eight degrees on Monday, sixty-six on Tuesday. Wednesday, lighter winds and partly sunny with a high of around sixty-eight. Currently we have fifty-six at JFK, sixty-four, mostly cloudy in Central Park, a south wind at five to ten. Repeating the current temperature sixty-four going down to fifty-six in midtown.

We'll continue to have that patchy, dense fog around the area this morning. That should burn off over the next couple of hours, then the next threat comes in this afternoon as we have some locally heavy thunderstorms that will move through the area, especially to the west of the city. We'll have a high today of about seventy degrees, evening showers, thunderstorms tonight, then clearing, breezy, turning cooler, with a low falling back to fifty-three. Both tomorrow and Tuesday will be windy with times of fog and sunshine, we could see a shower either day with highs in the mid-to-upper-sixties. And as we look ahead to Wednesday, a partly sunny, pleasant day with a high of sixty-eight. Dense fog at White Plains right now, fifty-six degrees, fifty-eight degrees at Islip, in Central Park, sixty-one degrees, relative humidity ninety-three percent, and the winds east, northeast at seven miles per hour. Repeating the current temperature sixty-one going up to seventy in midtown.

Well, a glance at the radar, not much out there, but a couple of showers most notable, just off to the south of Danbury, Connecticut and also, uh, kind of sandwiched in between the Garden State Parkway and 287, eh, coming down through, eh, Bergen, Passaic, as well as Essex, Morris counties, Union, in through that area. But again, it's more miss than hit. We'll have clouds and limited sun this afternoon, with the high of sixty-eight degrees. What we're going to notice tonight is the increase in the wind, lock, stock, and barrel, low temperature fifty-two degrees. And when I say it's a bad hair day tomorrow, that's an understatement on my part here. Clouds, limited sun, maybe an afternoon shower, forget the umbrella, high sixty-six. Wednesday will take the wind down a notch, partly sunny with the high sixty-eight. It's currently seventy Belmar, sixty with the clouds in Central Park, going to sixty-eight this afternoon in midtown.

We're starting out today OK with, uh, mixed clouds and sun. We think as the day wears on, there will tend to be more in the way of cloud cover. We're still under the circulation of a large storm system which is centered, uh, in northern New York state over the Adirondacks, and that could produce a shower or two as we go through this afternoon and this evening. Showers, mostly of the brief variety, high today sixty-four, then clearing late tonight, low fifty-two. Sunshine in pretty good supply tomorrow, should be a nice day, high sixty-eight, increasing clouds Thursday, and some rain again Thursday night and Friday. Right now it's fifty-two and partly sunny in Central Park, temperature today going up to sixty-four.

A better today, although it's not going to stay completely sunny. There will be cloudy intervals, and there will still be a cool breeze, but with the sun out at least at times, temperatures get into the sixties, probably the upper-sixties this afternoon. Then it'll be fair and cool tonight, low around fifty. Increasing clouds tomorrow, and we do look for some rain again as we get into tomorrow night, and during the day Friday. And a cool day Friday, with a breeze coming in off the ocean, temperatures only in the fifties. However, we are optimistic about improving weather for the weekend, gradual clearing Saturday, high sixty-two, and partly to mostly sunny on Sunday, high sixty-eight. Right now it's fifty-four, partly sunny in Central Park, temperature today going up to sixty-eight.

We still have sunshine and, uh, temperatures are getting into the sixties now and, although clouds will increase as we go through the afternoon, it'll still be comfortable with temperatures, uh, getting close to seventy, or at least on well up into the sixties. However, with the increasing clouds, the result of a storm which is in the Ohio Valley now, that storm is going to hit the eastern seaboard tomorrow and intensify and, around these parts, tomorrow is not looking like a nice day. Rain, some of it heavy, tomorrow and tomorrow night, ending Saturday morning. There'll also be gusty winds out of the east, they will be strong enough to raise concerns about some coastal flooding, at the time of high tide, tomorrow and tomorrow night. The atmosphere will dry Saturday afternoon, Sunday looks good, mostly sunny, with a high of sixty-eight. Right now it is sixty-two and sunny in Central Park, temperature today going up to sixty-eight.

Radar right now showing a little bit of light rain across Staten Island, on further south and west, and that'll be about where it stays for the overnight hours into the first part of tomorrow morning, a low forty-eight degrees. Then later tomorrow, still gusty winds, still fairly cold, drizzle to start, then little bit breaks of sunshine, a high around sixty. Lingering clouds and some late night fog tomorrow night, low forty-eight. Here comes the improvement on Sunday, turning out mostly sunny, noticeably milder, with a high of sixty-eight degrees. Plenty of sunshine on Monday with a high of seventy-four, and partly sunny and real nice on Tuesday, high seventy-six. Fifty-two right now in the Park, fifty-four in Newark, and fifty-three de . . . er, degrees at LaGuardia. Repeating the current temperature fifty-two going down to forty-eight in midtown.

Well, a few clouds lingering south and west of the city. Turned out to be a nice sunny afternoon, north and east, tonight no exception, uh, partly cloudy, uh, watch for some late night fog, though, a low of forty-six degrees. A nice day tomorrow, though, with plenty of sunshine and a high of sixty-eight. Mostly clear skies tomorrow night, low fifty-two, and another sunny day on Monday, with a high of seventy-four. Tuesday not looking too bad either, partly sunny with a high of seventy-four degrees. Right now in midtown fifty-nine degrees, northeast winds at nine miles per hour. Repeating the current temperature fifty-nine going down to forty-six in midtown.

It'll be mostly sunny and warm today, it's going up toward eighty. A little cooler in coastal areas, then increasing clouds tonight, low fifty-eight. Tomorrow, mostly cloudy with a couple of showers, as a cold front arrives, high seventy-two. Then behind the front, mostly cloudy and cooler. Thursday, there still could be a shower, high sixty-four. It's going to turn rainy at the end of the week for Friday and Saturday, temperatures in the fifties to low sixties at best. Currently winds out of the northeast at three miles per hour, beautifully sunny, relative humidity fifty percent, sixty-seven heading for eighty.

Well, uh, on this Tuesday evening, the radar showing a few showers to the west of the tri-state area, mainly around eastern and central Pennsylvania. These are associated with a cool front that will be approaching us tomorrow. And as it does, it'll be slowing down, and virtually stalling, along the eastern seaboard, and, of course, that doesn't bode well for our weather here for the remainder of the week. Temperatures tomorrow around seventy degrees, this despite clouds and a few showers and, uh, a wave of low pressure moving up from the southeastern United States, cruising along that nearly stationary front, I think that is what will have some very soggy implications for things around here, uh, Friday, and especially Friday night, uh. Temperatures Thursday expected to be no higher than the mid-sixties, that's well below normal, and then just as the Memorial Day weekend holiday gets started, the rain will be kicking in. Partly cloudy, sixty-five in midtown right now, relative humidity thirty-six percent, the wind light and variable. It's partly cloudy, sixty-five heading down to fifty-eight.

Well the rain has stopped from the city westbound, at least from midtown westbound, but we still find rain from Nassau eastbound, across Long Island. Looking live at the radar, I can tell that it'll be a while before the rain stops in those areas. We're gonna stay wet, at least damp early tonight, and late tonight, simply cloudy, we'll cool down to fifty-two. Mostly cloudy, breezy, cool weather tomorrow, rain could return to the area late in the day, a high of sixty, if not late in the day, then tomorrow night. We'll be dealing with the rain, that rain will continue Friday, Friday's high temperature only fifty-eight and, yes, unfortunately it looks like rain on Saturday as well, to kick off the holiday weekend, continued cool, somewhat windy, high of sixty degrees. Most of that rain should be over Sunday. Sunday mostly cloudy, high of sixty-six. Right now it's sixty, cloudy in Central Park, ninety-six percent humidity, winds variable at six miles per hour. Repeating the current temperature sixty going down to fifty-two in midtown.

Well, we have a damp night in the tri-state area, current radar showing most of the light rain over Long Island and, uh, coastal areas but, uh, actually a bit of drizzle occurring at all the airports right now, and it's cloudy in midtown. Temperatures, they're not going to change much overnight, fifty-one right now in midtown, we're heading down to fifty, and as we get the, uh, Friday started up, eh, the getaway day for the Memorial Day holiday weekend, more of this damp weather. We're waiting, actually, on a storm system organizing in Georgia right now to bring the real rain of consequence. Most of that should occur Friday night, and then Saturday it should stay dull and damp throughout much of the weekend, although we hold out hope for some brightening, uh, with, uh, Sunday afternoon and Monday rolling around. Right now cloudy, fifty-one in midtown, relative humidity one hundred percent, the wind northeast ten miles per hour. It's cloudy and fifty-one, heading down to fifty.

Well, for the rest of this afternoon, it'll be kind of dreary out there, lots of clouds, windy, cool, patchy fog, also intermittent rain and drizzle, with a high of fifty-eight degrees. Showers, drizzle lingers early tonight, maybe some clearing late, patchy fog continuing, well, falling back to fifty-four. For tomorrow, a warmer day, with clouds breaks and sunshine, could be a shower or thunderstorm in the afternoon, with a high of seventy-two degrees. Clouds, limited sunshine for Memorial Day, couple of showers and a thunderstorm possible, with a high of sixty-four, and a chance of a shower even lingers into Tuesday. Currently in Central Park, a cloudy sky, fifty-three degrees, relative humidity one hundred percent, and winds out of the east at fourteen miles per hour. Repeating the current temperature fifty-three going up to fifty-eight degrees in midtown.

Well, the rain has moved away from the area, however, we'll still have a lot of clouds around tonight, kind of a damp night, patchy fog will form with a low, falling back to about fifty. For Tuesday, a mostly cloudy day, could see an afternoon or nighttime shower. We'll have a high of sixty-six on Tuesday, low on Tuesday night of fifty-six. It continues mostly cloudy on Wednesday, couple of showers possible, high once again fifty-six degrees. And as we look ahead to Thursday, a little bit of sunshine, a little bit warmer, but still a chance of a shower or a thunderstorm, with a high of seventy-four degrees. Currently fifty-five degrees in Newark, in Central Park a cloudy sky, fifty-four degrees, relative humidity ninety-seven percent, and a wind variable at five miles per hour. Repeating the current temperature fifty-four going down to fifty in midtown.

We've got a very nice morning, certainly a lot better than yesterday looked at this time. As we go throughout the afternoon, we'll have an increase in cloudiness, not out of the question there's a shower, but basically, it's going to remain dry now. Tonight, showers are going to come in, most of them late tonight, the low fifty-six. Tomorrow will be a rainy day at times, high sixty-four at best, may stay in the low sixties. Thursday, though, cloudy to partly sunny and milder, could be an afternoon shower or thunderstorm, high seventy-four, then Friday, partly sunny and breezy, high seventy-eight degrees. Currently in midtown it's sixty-one, the relative humidity is seventy-two percent, the wind is light and variable, still sunny but it will turn cloudy for the afternoon. Sixty-one heading for sixty-eight.

Well, our radar not showing any significant rain, uh, around the metropolitan area at this point, there might be a sprinkle over the next few hours, but a little bit of a break. However there is another disturbance producing some rain in central Pennsylvania. The bulk of that will slide by to our south, but a couple of showers around here this afternoon and early this evening, and then clouds linger tonight. Tomorrow we look for breaks of sunshine and that'll get temperatures into the low, to maybe middle, seventies tomorrow. Couple of showers, maybe a thunderstorm tomorrow afternoon and night, and there may yet be a shower Friday morning. Then partly sunny, breezy, during the day Friday, high about seventy. Partly sunny Saturday, high into the seventies, but yet another chance of showers later Saturday or Saturday night. Right now it's fifty-seven and cloudy in Central Park, humidity is ninety-three percent, and the wind is calm. Repeating the current temperature fifty-seven going up to sixty-four today.

This time around we've got to flip up the expanded view of our radar. We are seeing the beginnings of thunder shower activity, but it's as far away as Poughkeepsie, so nothing close to home just yet, still more sunshine than clouds. We'll manage seventy-six for a high temperature, but it does go to show the fact that at least one or two neighborhoods can pick up a thunderstorm by this evening. Otherwise patchy clouds tonight, low fifty-eight. While tomorrow might start with a little bit of fog, I don't think it's going to be a scenario where we have to leave early to work or school. The balance of the day is going to be partly sunny and warm, so plan accordingly, high seventy-eight. Unfortunately, the clouds move in over the weekend, high seventy on Saturday, and starting Saturday afternoon, through the nighttime hours, it is a soaker. Right now seventy in Bridgeport, seventy-three and mostly sunny in Central Park, going to seventy-six this afternoon in midtown, so get out and enjoy it.

Nice day today. Beautiful. Sunshine. Afternoon temperature getting to about eighty. Then tonight, partly cloudy low sixty-two. Even tomorrow could start out OK, but then showers and thunderstorms will visit as a cold front approaches, low pressure area will be strengthening over us. Some of the rain could wind up being heavy, some of the thunderstorms could be gusty, tomorrow's high seventy, and some more showers tomorrow night. With a storm off-shore on Sunday, it'll turn into a windy cool day, plenty of cloudiness. There could be some showers left over, not out of the question, starts to clear late in the day, but the main theme is windy and cool, high sixty-eight. Then Monday things start to settle down, partly sunny, high seventy-four degrees. Currently it's sixty-three in midtown, relative humidity seventy-two percent, wind out of the north at five miles per hour. Sixty-three heading to seventy in time for lunch, and to eighty this afternoon.

Our radar shows, uh, a small but fairly intense thunderstorm, uh, just west of the city now, this is just southwest of Orange and into Union, and it's going to be following I-78, uh, right into, uh, Elizabeth, uh, clipping, uh, probably Jersey City and the upper portion of Staten Island in a few moments, uh, you can expect some brief, heavy downpours, uh, with this particular cell. Uh, smaller and lighter showers just about to move into White Plains, uh, heading east-ward, and that'll eventually get into Greenwich in a few moments, uh, so we've got a little action around here this afternoon and, uh, a little later on tonight, just partly cloudy skies, the low around sixty-two. Now, for tomorrow and tomorrow night, as a matter of fact, mostly cloudy skies, uh, showers, they will become more numerous as we get into the afternoon, uh, some heavier thunderstorms as well, and by the time this one's over, uh, we could have, uh, quite a dose of rain, uh, through Sunday morning, uh, probably three-quarters, to maybe an inch-and-a-half of water, temperatures near seventy tomorrow, mid-fifties tomorrow night. Sunday a very windy day on the back side of this storm, clouds, breaks of sun and a few more showers, the high only sixty-nine. Currently we have, uh, seventy-eight degrees with some sun in Central Park, a west wind at five. Repeating the current temperature seventy-eight going down to sixty-two in midtown.

Well, we've had a bit of a break over the last hour or so across the five boroughs, but there are more showers coming our way from, uh, central New Jersey and eastern Pennsylvania. There's still rain up the Hudson Valley, there's still rain in Connecticut, there's still rain on Suffolk County and eastern Nassau. So it's going to be a wet evening, and a wet night, some of the rain heavy enough to produce street and highway flooding, and a flood watch remains in effect for areas north and west of the city. Tomorrow morning will be rainy and windy, the rain will end around midday, but the wind will continue to be strong and gusty all day tomorrow, upwards of forty miles per hour, even higher. Slowly diminishing wind tomorrow night, and Monday and Tuesday will be much nicer days, with sunshine and temperatures back into the seventies. Right now it's sixty-one and mostly cloudy in Central Park, temperature tonight going down to fifty-six.

Well, the flash flood watch continues until eleven forty-one this morning for pretty much all of the area west and north of New York City. We're seeing some urban and street and highway flooding even, in and around the city as well as, uh, heavy rain is in the area, and we have a flood warning for the Mahwah River, up around Suffern, New York. So, uh, all kinds of, uh, wonderful stuff going on this morning, with all of the rain and wind. We'll see things begin to abate this afternoon, the rain letting up, in fact, it'll end by late this afternoon, the high sixty-four. Windy, chilly tonight, down to fifty-four. Tomorrow and Tuesday, a couple of very nice days, a high in the mid-seventies. Right now, some rain, fifty-eight in Central Park, repeating the current temperature fifty-eight going up to sixty-four.

And it's a forecast that contains rain once again. Another storm is, uh, moving across Missouri right now puttin' down a lot of water across, uh, Illinois, and this system is going to be tracking, due east the next, uh, forty-eight hours, moving across Kentucky, West Virginia and Virginia, oh, but that's close enough, and it's gonna deliver some rain here once again. Overnight, though, it's mostly clear and comfortable, and Tuesday is a nice day with sunshine, uh, fading behind the clouds with a high of seventy. Rain comes in tomorrow evening, continues rather steadily throughout the night, a low of fifty-two. Wednesday, a cloudy, cool, day with off-and-on rain and drizzle, a high of sixty-three, and by Thursday, the system will be well offshore. The clouds will break for some sunshine once again, and will warm things back up, seventy-four on Thursday, Friday partly sunny and seventy-eight. Currently sixty-nine degrees, a clear sky in Central Park, the wind west at seven to fourteen miles per hour. Repeating the current temperature sixty-nine, going down to fifty-six in midtown.

Mostly cloudy for a time this evening. Partly cloudy overnight, and no rain to talk about, for a change, a low of fifty-eight degrees and, in fact, tomorrow will turn out quite pleasant, with a good deal of sunshine. Noticeably warmer, with a high near eighty tomorrow afternoon, although cooler near the beaches. Clear early tomorrow night, increasing clouds late at night, a low of sixty-four. We're back to mostly cloudy skies Saturday, looks like showers and a thunderstorm or two during the afternoon, high of seventy-two degrees. Drying out on Sunday, and a mix of clouds and sun, high of seventy-four, maybe a shower or two Monday, and a high of seventy-two. Right now, sixty-nine and cloudy in Central Park, fifty-four percent humidity, a west wind at ten miles per hour, gusting to eighteen miles per hour. Repeating the current temperature sixty-nine going down to fifty-eight in midtown.

Well, I just can't find anything bad with today's weather here, still lots of sunshine, temperatures gradually approaching eighty degrees midtown, cooler coastal Connecticut, and on Long Island, of course, but, uh, even as we head on into tonight, it stays dry. Clear skies will make way for more clouds after midnight, a low of sixty-four degrees midtown, fifty-eight throughout the suburbs. That's not bad. Unfortunately, if you're headed out and about over the course of the weekend, hey, it's the, uh, summer holiday season, seventy-two degrees with a lot of cloud cover tomorrow. Keep in mind you'll need the, uh, well the babushkas, the ponchos, the, er, ra, well, the Paddington Bear weather gear, starting tomorrow afternoon, and you know what, all kidding aside, late tomorrow, tomorrow night, the possibility of flooding does exist with this nasty storm. Sunday could start off damp, otherwise it turns partly sunny, breezy, high seventy-six. Right now seventy-two Islip, seventy-three with the sun in Central Park, we'll manage eighty this afternoon in midtown.

A little cloudiness for the balance of the morning, this afternoon the clouds may break, allowing temperatures to get into the mid-seventies, to about seventy-six, clear tonight low sixty-four. Tomorrow should be a sunny, warm day, high eighty-two. A front now crossing the Plains states may trigger a couple of showers and thunderstorms during the day Wednesday, high eighty, before that system moves offshore Thursday. That day should be partly sunny, high seventy-eight. Currently in midtown sixty degrees, the relative humidity is seventy-five percent, still cloudy, heading for seventy-six this afternoon.

Hey, it's a beautiful morning, and it's gonna stay nice and bright and sunny all day long today, and temperatures get to eighty and above from, uh, midtown on across the river and into adjacent New Jersey. It'll be a little cooler right at the shore, but still nice and sunny. Tonight partly cloudy and mild, with a low in the sixties. Tomorrow, more in the way of clouds, and the humidity returns as well, so there can be a shower tomorrow, maybe afternoon thunderstorms, high near eighty. Partly sunny weather returns for Thursday, that should be a nice day, high seventy-four, and then a shower possibility back into the scene for Friday and Saturday, but right now, it is sixty-seven and bright and sunny in Central Park, humidity sixty-two percent, wind from the west at nine. Repeating the current temperature sixty-seven going up to eighty-two today.

Well, dew points are well into the sixties at this hour around the region, that's an indication of how humid it is. Those high dew points will help fuel more showers and a thunderstorm around the tri-state as we head through the afternoon hours. Currently, I see some showers north of the Tappan Zee, and across a good bit of Connecticut, but little rain across New Jersey. Our high this afternoon will approach eighty, rain at times and muggy tonight and tomorrow, even a thunderstorm or two, maybe even some flooding problems, the low sixty-six. High tomorrow seventy-four, cooler on Long Island and in Connecticut. Lots of clouds, maybe a little sun at times over the weekend, but still a chance for a shower each day, especially Saturday, high both days seventy-four. Right now seventy-three in White Plains and Islip, seventy-four, mostly cloudy in Central Park, relative humidity seventy-five percent, winds west at five miles per hour. Repeating the current temperature seventy-four going up to eighty in midtown.

And, what we have here is, uh, very humid conditions for the nighttime hours, uh, temperatures only dipping back into the mid-sixties. Uh, it has been, uh, quiet on the radar, uh, we did have quite a bit of rain north of the city all day long, and the rain is now starting to show up, uh, to our southwest, this is getting into the, uh, Harrisburg, Lancaster area. Heavy thunderstorms out in Washington and Baltimore, and it's all pushing northeastward toward us. Uh, we are expecting to see periods of rain late tonight and tomorrow, even a thunderstorm, uh, temperatures tomorrow in the low to mid-seventies. Tomorrow night, uh, leftover showers or thunderstorms, and as we go through the weekend, uh, improving conditions. Saturday is a transition day, uh, we'll see clouds break for some sun, but there still could be a shower or thunderstorm, but Sunday should be partly sunny and seventy-four, and then lots of sunshine on Monday. Currently cloudy skies, seventy-seven degrees, an east wind at seven. Repeating the current temperature seventy-seven going down to sixty-six in midtown.

Well, our flood watch continues in effect until midnight for Rockland, Bergen, Essex, Passaic, and Union counties, but the radar not really showing much of anything out there. A lot of cloud cover, uh, there's the shower here and there, along with the spot of drizzle, but seventy-four degrees. That's not all that bad. High humidity, temperatures running in the sixties for Long Island and Connecticut. Late this afternoon throughout the, uh, first part of the nighttime hours, this is our best bet to pick up a heavier thunderstorm, later on tonight just be cautious about fog, low sixty-eight. But honestly, tomorrow's not much of a change, clouds, a little bit of sun, still warm and humid, we're up at eighty degrees, but still, the threat of a shower and thunderstorms primarily during the midday and the afternoon. It's on Sunday that we finally dry things out with the high near eighty. Right now it's sixty-seven degrees Newark, sixty-three with the clouds in Central Park, going up to seventy-four this afternoon in midtown.

Uh, gray skies tonight, humid conditions, areas of dense fog, drizzle. On top of that a coupla showers, even an evening thunderstorm, uh, right now we have some thunderstorms over southeastern Pennsylvania, working their way slowly northeastward toward us. Uh, temperatures, uh, steady, we're slowly rising, we're gonna be up in the middle-sixties at daybreak. Tomorrow the, uh, frontal boundary, which is stalled on top of this, will have drifted back up to our north and, on a southwest breeze, it's gonna be a much warmer day, eighty-three with the high temperature, uh, clouds, uh, little bit of sunshine, but, uh, another shower or thunderstorm is a good bet in the afternoon and evening, uh, as one last wave of low pressure comes eastward from the Ohio Valley. Behind that, we will finally build in high pressure for a few days, uh, Sunday will be partly sunny at eighty, Monday and Tuesday lots of sunshine, temperatures in the upper-seventies. Cloudy skies, sixty degrees in Central Park, ninety-six percent humidity, and a northeast wind at thirteen. Repeating the current temperature sixty and holding steady or slowly rising in midtown tonight.

Yeah, that there is, uh, we have, uh, a couple of, uh, very strong thunderstorm cells north of the city right now. Uh, the, uh, closest one, eh, actually due north of the city, this is near the Tappan Zee Bridge, actually or, or just north of there, and extends, uh, westward, uh, back into, well, right along the, uh, Morris, uh, Sussex County line, this will be north of Rockaway, uh, probably, uh, six to eight miles to the north, northwest of there, uh, but a couple of those cells are extremely intense, uh, causing frequent cloud-to-ground lightning and, uh, some torrential downpours. Ah, the line moving towards the east, southeast at about twenty-five miles an hour, uh, so areas that are effected, it's going to be moving through much of Bergen county, uh, it will also be hitting, uh, much of central and southern Westchester Country and maybe getting down into, uh, the Bronx, uh, it's probably going to take another, uh, twenty, twenty to twenty-five minutes or so for it to, uh, reach the northern side of the city. Uh, we do have a severe thunderstorm watch until seven p.m. for all of, uh, New Jersey. Uh, we'll call it a very humid evening, uh, with a couple of showers and heavy thunderstorms moving through the region late tonight, just partly cloudy, and then on the other side of this front, some nice weather, tomorrow, Monday, and Tuesday. Uh, it's not until Wednesday that we, uh, mention a shower once again. Currently seventy-five degrees, with some hazy sun, and a southwest breeze eight to sixteen miles an hour. Repeating the current temperature seventy-five going up to eighty-three in midtown.

Those who were stressed by the fact that it's been dry for, oh, almost, uh, eighteen, twenty hours, uh, well, rest assured, rain has returned. We'll have rain at times today and tonight. There's a flood watch through tomorrow morning for Morris, Warren, Sussex, Hunterdon, Somerset, and Monmouth counties in New Jersey. Others may be added depending on how heavy the rain is tonight and tomorrow morning. Today's high seventy-four, low tonight sixty-four, and for tomorrow and Saturday, cloudy and cool, periods of rain, high sixty-seven both days. Sunday, ending rain in the morning will finally depart, give away to clearing, high seventy-two, and much warmer weather next week. Currently in midtown with some rain, relative humidity is eighty-nine percent, the air is calm, sixty-eight degrees heading for seventy-four.

There is rain around the metropolitan area now, uh, most of it to the west and north of, uh, Manhattan, but, uh, it will become more widespread and prevalent as we go through the day today. We'll have rain a good part of the time tonight, and tomorrow, and tomorrow night, and into Sunday morning. Parts of our area could get more than two or three inches of rain, primarily north and west of the city, and there is concern about flooding, and flood watches are in effect. The atmosphere will begin drying out during the afternoon on Sunday and, uh, the Mets and Yankees have a chance of getting in Sunday night's game, not much of a chance we don't think, tonight or tomorrow, Monday, Tuesday, Wednesday, of next week, though, sunny and much warmer, well on up into the eighties. Right now sixty-five and cloudy in Central Park, temperature today going up only to sixty-eight.

SUMMER

Well, what we can see here is the scattering of showers across much of the tri-state area, maybe between New York City, and now westward. This coverage will increase as we head through the afternoon, it will become heavy at times, as well, late in the day and at night. As a result, we have a flood watch out for just about the entire tri-state area, except for eastern Long Island and eastern Connecticut. We'll have a high today only of sixty-five, low tonight falling back to fifty-eight. A couple of leftover showers tomorrow, with the high of seventy-four degrees, then it turns mostly sunny and warmer on Monday and Tuesday, with highs both days in the upper-eighties. Currently some light rain falling in Newark, in Central Park we have a cloudy sky, sixty-two degrees, relative humidity seventy-seven percent, and a wind out of the east at fourteen, gusting to eighteen miles per hour. Repeating the current temperature sixty-two going up to sixty-five in midtown.

We are going to continue to see showery weather over the next twelve to twenty-four hours. The good news is, eventually, and, well, soon, some much nicer weather. As soon as tomorrow, we are going to see beautiful, warmer weather with sunshine, we hit the mid-eighties tomorrow, but upper-eighties by Tuesday. Wednesday, believe it or not, ninety degrees is what we're forecasting for midtown, the humidity comes up, so while it will be nice and sunny, it won't necessarily be comfortable. The south shore of Long Island and coastal Connecticut will likely stay in the mid-eighties. Sixty-one at Newark, sixty at LaGuardia, and fifty-nine at JFK right now. It's fifty-nine in the Park, cloudy in New York, the relative humidity ninety-three percent, winds light and variable, fifty-nine now, we'll go to seventy in midtown today.

It will be a sunny to partly cloudy day today, as temperatures warm into the eighties this afternoon. And it's clear tonight, the low about sixty-five. Sunny tomorrow, getting close to ninety, and then into the nineties with the humidity starting to build up Wednesday and Thursday, could even be some ninety-four's or ninety-six's showing up in the interior hot spots Wednesday and Thursday, so an early summer heat wave. Next chance for a shower or thunderstorm comes on about Friday. Right now it is sixty-five and sunny in Central Park, temperature today going up to eighty-three.

Temperatures in most places riding about two or three degrees above the pace of yesterday, and in Central Park yesterday, we topped out at ninety-three, so a ninety-six or thereabouts this afternoon, uh, seems like a pretty good representative number, but it could get to one hundred in some of the interior hot spots around Morristown and Caldwell and Newark this afternoon. And tomorrow, a similar day, and that RealFeel temperature will be up over one hundred. By the time we get to Friday, a cold front will be approaching that could produce a thunderstorm in the afternoon. The weekend, the humidity drops, the temperature should be trimmed by several degrees, highs in the eighties, and both days should be at least partly sunny. Right now, though, it's eighty-one and sunny in Central Park, and the temperature today going up to ninety-six.

Today probably the hottest day of the week, the hottest day of this heat wave, uh, and, uh, a real sizzler, and because of the sunshine and the heat, uh, and, uh, a lack of wind, that combines to produce, eh, ozone, a combination of oxygen and sulfur compounds that are produced, uh, a lot by automobile exhaust, and so we have, uh, an ozone alert in effect. If you're sensitive to that kind of thing, take it easy, otherwise, you want to take it easy anyway, because it'll be ninety-six or ninety-eight degrees this afternoon. Tomorrow, partly sunny, still hot and humid, maybe an afternoon thunderstorm, and then we get a nice break for the weekend. The sun returns Saturday maybe after some morning clouds, the humidity lowers, the high eighty-six, and partly to mostly sunny on Sunday, the high eighty-four. Right now it is seventy-nine and sunny in Central Park, and the temperature today going up to a sizzling ninety-six.

There is relief on the way, but for the rest of the day today, it's going to be hazy and hot. Sunshine will mix with some clouds as we go through the afternoon, but the temperature gets into the nineties anyway, and maybe there's a thunderstorm this afternoon as a front passes through. It'll clear behind that tonight, temperatures drop into the sixties, and a nice day tomorrow, warm enough to be outside for the beach, eighty-four, but the humidity down enough to make it comfortable. Clouds and sun on Sunday with a high of eighty-two. There's a slight chance for a shower Sunday, better chance to hold off till Sunday night or Monday. Right now, uh, we have sunshine, it's eighty-one degrees in Central Park, the temperature today going up to ninety-three.

Well, you can already feel that heat and humidity out there as the sun, uh, has been really warming us up and, uh, we'll stay that way today. Some clouds and parts of the area could get a thunderstorm this afternoon or early tonight, as a cold front passes through, but not all of us seeing any shower activity, a high of eighty-eight, clear tonight, a low of sixty-eight. Sunshine tomorrow and Wednesday, highs in the mid-to-upper-eighties, with fairly comfortable humidity levels. And hot and more humid Thursday, and also the Fourth of July, with highs back up around the ninety degree mark. Right now we have seventy-five at Morristown, it's seventy-four at Islip, mostly sunny and seventy-five in . . . seventy-six that is, in Central Park, west wind at six, and eighty-two percent humidity. Seventy-six going up to eighty-eight today.

Mostly clear, comfortable conditions tonight, and another nice day coming up tomorrow, sunshine, some high clouds starting to move in, afternoon temperatures low to middle-eighties. Those clouds will lower and thicken tomorrow night, and then we're, uh, we've got a shot of seeing some showers late tomorrow night and Thursday. Those are remains of tropical storm Bill, uh, that's, uh, pushing northeastward right now into extreme northwestern portions of Georgia, uh, with the rain already up into, uh, southern and central portions of Virginia this hour, uh, so we could see a bit of rain out of that, uh, late tomorrow night and Thursday. And then for Friday, the Fourth, and Saturday, it looks hot and humid as that system heads out to sea, partly sunny skies, afternoon temperatures in the low nineties. We have eighty degrees under a mostly clear sky in Central Park, a southwest breeze at ten, repeating the current temperature eighty, going down to sixty-eight in midtown.

Well, we are watching some rain on our radar, most of it, uh, is east and south of the city, central and southern New Jersey, and also the south shore of Suffolk County, but they are a couple of little sprinkles, a couple of little drizzles, scattered around. During the middle of the day in the afternoon, clouds will thin out, there'll be some sun, temperatures get into the lower eighties. Then tomorrow it turns, uh, hot and humid, with hazy sunshine, and the high in the low nineties. And a similar day on Saturday, although late Saturday there could be a shower or a thunderstorm, as a weak front passes through. Behind that front it's still hot Sunday, it's still sunny, but the humidity should lower pretty noticeably in the Sunday, Monday, time period, high temperatures those days around ninety. Right now it is seventy-one and cloudy in Central Park, temperature today going up to eighty-two.

Partly cloudy, warm, humid conditions overnight, and a hot, steamy day coming up tomorrow, a good deal of sunshine with afternoon readings in the middle-nineties, our RealFeel reading, though, might reach one hundred to one hundred and five. It's gonna be warm and stuffy tomorrow night, seventy-eight for a low, with a cold front finally arriving on the scene Wednesday with thunderstorms, uh, one more hot, humid day, however, temperatures getting near ninety degrees. That'll be it for the rest of the week, uh, Thursday it's only in the mid-seventies, mostly cloudy skies, a few showers. Showers still a possibility Friday morning before clearing out, the high temperature near eighty, and it looks like the weekend should be pretty nice. We have seventy-seven degrees and a partly cloudy sky in Central Park, west wind at eight. Repeating the current temperature seventy-seven going down to seventy-four in midtown.

We're going to have a hot day today, the temperature climbing through the rest of the seventies in the next hour or so, getting to eighty-five to ninety degrees in time for lunch, and then into the nineties for the afternoon, the projected high temperature ninety-six, and we'll have high humidity. The wind'll pick up a little bit out of the west, won't help that much, though. Thunderstorm chance is quite low today. Then tonight quite warm, only dropping to seventy-eight. Tomorrow very warm, humid, clouds and sunshine, a couple of thunderstorms, especially in the afternoon and evening, high eighty-eight. Thursday looks to be cooler, plenty of cloudiness, a high seventy-eight. Friday, cloudy to partly sunny with a thunderstorm or two, the high eighty degrees. Currently in midtown seventy-seven, the relative humidity eighty-one percent, wind light and variable. Partly sunny seventy-seven, heading for ninety-six.

Well, it's humid, but it's not so hot, with the clouds this afternoon, high temperature eighty-four degrees. As a matter of fact, some areas picking up a shower or thunderstorm, most notably over parts of Suffolk County, but also one now developing for our radar, along the part of 280, stretching out over Essex County, all of it moving off to the east, southeast. Once again, we'll manage eighty-four this afternoon, still a shower, thunderstorm around early tonight, then partial clearing late with the low of sixty-eight degrees. Tomorrow mostly cloudy and even cooler, believe it or not, with the high of seventy-eight, although it still could shower in the afternoon. Oh ho! Come tomorrow night and Friday, we get soaked! Friday's high eighty-two. Right now, it's eighty-six Newark, eighty-three with clouds, Central Park managing only eighty-four this afternoon in midtown.

Cloudiness, there can be a few sunny breaks, there can be a shower from time to time. It's not going to be a cold day, but it's a lot cooler than it's been recently, sixty-seven currently, turning to seventy-four this afternoon. A few showers and a thunderstorm likely tonight into tomorrow, low tonight sixty-six. Then tomorrow afternoon, clouds and sunshine with a high eighty-two, could be a thunderstorm late tomorrow or tomorrow night, the low seventy. Then things should settle down for the weekend, Saturday partly to mostly sunny and less humid, high eighty-four, Sunday mostly sunny, high eighty-six degrees. Currently it's sixty-seven, relative humidity eighty-six percent, winds out of the east, northeast at eight, plenty of cloudiness, shower here and there, sixty-seven heading for seventy-four.

Well, in most areas the rain has moved on. We still find some shower activity over Suffolk County, Long Island, northbound into parts of Connecticut, but even there the rain will stop within the next hour or so. We're gonna be left with a partly cloudy night, low temperature tonight overnight at sixty-eight degrees. Tomorrow, a pretty good start to the weekend, sunshine, some clouds, a warm breeze, but not as humid as today, with a high of eighty-four degrees. Dry and comfortable tomorrow night, clear to partly cloudy, low sixty in the suburbs and sixty-eight in midtown. Sunday, a mixture of clouds and sunshine, a high again of eighty-four. Now, there could be a shower or thunderstorm some point Sunday night and Monday, otherwise for Monday, partly cloudy to partly sunny, high eighty-two. Partly sunny, warm, a little more humid on Tuesday, and a high of eighty-four. Right now it's seventy-two, mostly cloudy in Central Park, winds to the west at three miles per hour, one hundred percent humidity. Repeating the current temperature seventy-two going down to sixty-eight in midtown.

It'll be mostly cloudy today and tonight, a couple of showers and a thunderstorm, the high seventy-eight, tonight's low near sixty-eight. Tomorrow, humid with changing amounts of clouds and sun, as well as a chance for a shower or thunderstorm, high eighty-four. All this caused by the action of warm, humid air climbing over the retreating, slightly drier air that we had during the weekend. Wednesday, as a weak cool front approaches, warm and humid, with times of clouds and sunshine, a thunderstorm possible, high eighty-eight. Behind the front, not much temperature change, but probably less humid for Thursday, partly sunny, high eighty-six. Currently it's seventy-two, the relative humidity eighty-seven percent, wind light and variable, seventy-two heading for seventy-eight.

We started with some low clouds and fog in many areas this morning, but now we're seeing sunshine in most places, and it's going to warm up nicely into the mid-eighties this afternoon. A partly cloudy start to the night, then clouds will increase late at night, with a low near seventy. A front will cross the area tomorrow, with it some clouds, some intervals of sun, and the chance for a thunderstorm. It'll be very warm tomorrow, with a high in the upper-eighties, then behind that front some rather tranquil weather on Thursday, a mix of sun and clouds, high eighty-six. About the same Friday, maybe a thunderstorm at some point before the day is through on Friday. Currently seventy-five at JFK and at LaGuardia, seventy-four and partly sunny in Central Park, relative humidity eighty-one percent, the air is calm. Repeating the current temperature seventy-four going up to eighty-four in midtown.

We played down the shower, and we're mentioning just a brief shower in a few spots this morning. There are a few scattered across northwestern New Jersey, a batch went across the Rockland, Westchester County area a few hours ago, and are now in central Connecticut, but most areas getting nothing. Maybe a thunderstorm occurs late this afternoon, this evening, as a cool front arrives ahead of it, going to eighty-four. Partly cloudy later tonight, the low seventy. Tomorrow partly sunny, less humid, a fine day, high eighty-six. Friday, times of clouds and sunshine, a slight chance for a shower or thunderstorm as the next cold front approaches, high eighty-six, not much cooling behind it, though. Saturday some sunshine and some clouds, high eighty-four degrees. Currently in midtown it's seventy-three, the relative humidity is eighty-five percent, wind light and variable, seventy-three heading for eighty-four.

It's been sunny so far, it'll stay that way all day, going to eighty-six this afternoon, with low humidity. Clear to partly cloudy tonight, low seventy-two. Tomorrow there'll be an increase in cloudiness and also humidity, a shower or thunderstorm could occur as a weak cool front approaches from the northwest. Best chance for that is in the afternoon, high eighty-four. And behind the front, uh, a day like today on Saturday, it appears partly to mostly sunny, high eighty-four degrees. Then the humidity increases again on Sunday, warm and humid, a mixture of clouds and sunshine, high eighty-six. Currently, it's seventy-one degrees in midtown, relative humidity sixty-eight percent, wind out of the north at six miles per hour, seventy-one heading for eighty-six this afternoon.

There are a few showers that'll pass just to the north of the city in the next hour or two, but the next batch is not coming until later. So we're gonna say that the best chance of the showers and thunderstorms will be later on this afternoon and this evening. Anything before that would be just a hit or miss kind of thing, temperature today going well up into the eighties, in any case. Then tonight things settle back to the seventy degree mark. Tomorrow we're expecting, uh, a mixture of clouds and sunshine, slight chance of a thunderstorm, could be that all the moisture is offshore, the high eighty-two. Sunday looks like a fine day, sunny, warm, rather humid, high eighty-six degrees, standard mid-to-late July weather. Monday variable cloudiness, warm and humid, a couple of showers and thunderstorms, the high eighty-six. Currently in midtown, with sunshine, seventy-four degrees, relative humidity sixty-six percent, wind out of the west, southwest at nine miles per hour, seventy-four heading to eighty-four.

We're going to have some showers and thunderstorms forming around the area during the course of the day, although nothing is imminent right now, and it appears that most places are not going to get anything until this afternoon or this evening, whereupon there will be some showers and thunderstorms, today's high near eighty-two, backing down to only seventy-two tonight. Any shower or thunderstorm that forms tonight, tomorrow, or through Wednesday can be heavy, but again, the majority of the time, it won't actually be raining, tomorrow's high eighty-two, Wednesday's high eighty. Thursday mostly cloudy and humid, there still can be a shower or thunderstorm, the high eighty-four degrees. Currently in midtown the relative humidity is ninety-five percent, the wind is out of the south at seven miles per hour, seventy-one degrees in midtown, heading for eighty-two.

It is going to rain, but the important thing to keep in mind is even when it does rain, it can really pour, it can be a lot of lightning, thunder, and strong winds. The actual number of hours that it rains in a given twelve-hour period, usually less than two, so, most of the time you can go about regular activities, just keep an eye on the sky, and an ear right here. Going to eighty-two today, down to seventy tonight, up to eighty tomorrow. Thursday clouds and sunshine, a shower or thunderstorm, high eighty-four. Then Friday, partly sunny and warm, high eighty-six degrees. Currently we see no showers upstream from us, to the south and west, there are some in central Connecticut, retreating to the northeast. Currently in midtown seventy-one, relative humidity one hundred percent, wind south at six, seventy-one heading for eighty-two.

Showers and, uh, a couple of thunderstorms are still in the area, but the back edge is moving northeastward across central New Jersey. If it holds together, these showers will be out of the way by nine o'clock or so. There are a couple of small showers showing up to the southwest of there, so it may not be totally dry the rest of the morning, but probably nothing heavy. Showers and thunderstorms, potentially damaging and potentially flooding, though, can occur later this afternoon and again tonight. Today's high temperature eighty degrees . . . sounds like I'm underwater . . . eighty degrees, going down to seventy tonight, then up to eighty tomorrow. We expect sunshine to increase on Friday and Saturday, much less chance of any rain, afternoon temperature in the eighties. Currently in midtown seventy-one degrees, relative humidity one hundred percent, going up to eighty this afternoon.

Well, so far so good here this afternoon, our radar not picking up any activity. We still have, uh, this front, however, in the region, so there is at least a possibility that, uh, a few spots could see a shower or thunderstorm this afternoon or early evening. Otherwise, partly sunny, humid, low eighties for a high temperature, and tonight just a few clouds, maybe a bit of fog forming in some of the suburbs late tonight, seventy in midtown, with sixties in the suburbs. And then for the next couple of days, uh, this boundary is finally out of here, uh, we're just left with, uh, a ridge of high pressure giving us, uh, sunshine and warm weather, eighty-six tomorrow, ninety-two degrees on Saturday. Sunday looks to be a breezy, very warm, humid day with some sunshine, could see an afternoon or evening thunderstorm as the front does approach. Currently seventy-nine in Caldwell, seventy-six degrees and sunshine in Central Park, a southwest breeze at nine. Repeating the current temperature seventy-six going up to eighty-two in midtown.

Well, after all the showers and even severe weather that we've had this week, calm weather is certainly welcome. It's going to be gorgeous with sunshine, low humidity, and a high of eighty-eight degrees this afternoon. It'll be clear tonight, low seventy-two. Hot and becoming more humid tomorrow, mostly sunny, a high of ninety-two, and a real scorcher for Sunday, humidity, and a high of ninety-four. Now there could be a thunderstorm late in the day or at night on Sunday, then it'll be cooler and less humid, with some sunshine on Monday. Right now we have seventy-one at Caldwell, at Islip it's seventy-two, it's sunny in Central Park, sixty-eight percent humidity, and a calm wind. Seventy-two right now going up to eighty-eight.

Tonight will be warm and humid, the skies will stay clear, low seventy-six degrees. Ah, it'll stay muggy tomorrow, with a mix of clouds and sun. There's a chance of a thunderstorm late tomorrow as well as tomorrow night, high ninety-four through the afternoon, and tomorrow night's low seventy-eight degrees. Monday, clouds and sun, not as warm, there's still the chance of a thunderstorm, especially south of the city. Monday's high eighty-five, and then Tuesday and Wednesday will bring clouds and sun, and possibly a thunderstorm either day, Tuesday's high eighty, and Wednesday's high eighty-two. Eighty-six degrees right now in Central Park, the winds are west at seven miles per hour, fifty-one percent relative humidity, it's eighty-eight at both LaGuardia airport and in Newark.

We're still watching one or two little light showers on the radar into central and southern New Jersey, but for the most part, though, the tri-state area today will be a dry day. Sun, uh, mixed with clouds and, uh, not as hot as yesterday, not nineties today, but middle-eighties, uh, generally, and then fair tonight, low seventy or so in the city, but into the sixties in many suburbs. Partly to mostly sunny tomorrow, high eighty-two. Mostly sunny Wednesday, the high eighty-four. Next chance of showers and thunderstorms comes, uh, Thursday and also into Friday. Right now it is seventy-seven and mostly sunny in Central Park, temperature today going up to eighty-four.

Just some scattered high clouds today, otherwise it will be a mostly sunny day, and temperatures get to the low eighties, and the humidity, eh, under control so that eighty-two this afternoon should be pretty tolerable. And a clear, comfortable night tonight, low sixty-six in midtown, sixty in many suburbs, even, the uh, well, middle-fifties in some of the coolest northern and western suburbs, so a nice night for the middle of summer. Tomorrow mostly sunny, high eighty-four, sun followed by clouds Thursday, high again eighty-four, and we start to pick up the chance for a shower or thunderstorm Friday, and that chance stays with us Saturday and probably Sunday. Right now it is seventy and mostly sunny in Central Park, and the temperature today going up to eighty-two.

Well, it's definitely been a very nice start to the week, uh, you're gonna love this afternoon, but then things begin to change. Well, we'll give you the good news first. Sunshine, nice this afternoon, high about eighty-four. Clear to partly cloudy tonight, a low of sixty-eight, and moisture begins to return from the south tomorrow, so sun will give way to clouds. It'll become more humid in the afternoon with a high of eighty. A shower tomorrow night, then, uh, a shower or thunderstorm at anytime, and more humid Friday and Saturday, up to eighty on Friday, and about eighty-four on Saturday. Right now it's seventy-six at White Plains, seventy-five at Bridgeport, mostly sunny and seventy-eight in Central Park, fifty-seven percent humidity, and a south wind at three. It's seventy-eight and it's going up to eighty-four today.

Well, a gusty wind and the humidity are two factors that, uh, go against the good hair day this afternoon. We'll have clouds, sun, high temperature eighty-one degrees, but more cloud cover even tonight. But if there's a shower, that's well after midnight, low temperature sixty-eight degrees. And that's pretty much a similar bet tomorrow morning, maybe a brief shower here and there, otherwise mostly cloudy. Now, starting tomorrow afternoon, uh, more numerous showers then a thunderstorm, so this is where you're definitely gonna need the umbrella, with a high temperature of seventy-six degrees. Over the weekend, the balance of the time it's going to be sunny, warm, humid, highs of eighty-four and eighty-six. Yes, there will be a thunderstorm but, I tell you what, at least seventy-five to eighty-five percent of the weekend rain-free, so don't cancel outdoor plans yet. It's seventy-three in West Hampton, seventy-nine, mostly sunny in Central Park, going to eighty-one this afternoon in midtown.

We have a lot of cloudiness today. There can be a shower from time to time, most of the time just the clouds, a little bit of drizzle, it's going up to seventy-six, humid tonight, a shower or thunderstorm, low seventy. The weekend, changeable, sometimes the sun'll be out, it'll get warmer than today, going to eighty-two tomorrow, eighty-six on Sunday, but parts of the area will also get a thunderstorm each day, so keep an eye on the sky, and an ear right here as those approach. Monday and Tuesday, more of the same kind of weather, the pattern not really changing that much. Currently in midtown it's seventy-one degrees and cloudy, the relative humidity is one hundred percent, winds out of the southwest, five miles per hour, seventy-one heading to seventy-six.

Yeah, it sure is, and it's another, uh, day in which we're concerned about the possibility of some heavy, uh, rainfall but not immediately. Still looking at our radar, I don't see any significant rain around the area, even a few little minor breaks in the cloud cover, but later this afternoon, tonight, and tomorrow, an upper air disturbance comes overhead and helps to squeeze out some additional moisture. Showers and thunderstorms could be very heavy and a flood watch, uh, is in effect for most of our area. Thursday and Friday should bring some sun, highs in the eighties and muggy, and there can still be a shower or thunderstorm. Right now it is seventy-five degrees, uh, and mostly cloudy in Central Park, temperature today going up to eighty-two.

For a change, we're not talking about a lot of thunderstorms popping up in midday as we have the past two or three afternoons, but there can still be one or two of them around, but again, a much less active afternoon around the tri-state than what we've grown accustomed to earlier this week. Still it'll be warm and humid, with clouds and sun, and a high of eighty-four. Tonight it's humid, uh, a leftover shower or thunderstorm, mainly early, low seventy-two. Tomorrow, much like today, partly sunny, warm and humid, but watch for a shower and thunderstorm in the afternoon, the high eighty-four. Looks like Friday will be the most active day for the rest of the week, better chance for showers and thunderstorms, the high eighty-two. Then for Saturday, some intervals of sunshine, warm and humid, maybe a thunderstorm much like today, Saturday's high eighty-four. It's eighty-one in Morristown now, and seventy-nine at Teterboro, seventy-five and partly sunny in Central Park, relative humidity eighty-seven percent, the wind is variable at five miles per hour. Repeating the current temperature seventy-five going up to eighty-four in midtown.

Our weather's going to deteriorate as the day progresses. Looking at our radar right now, we see an area of rain and thunderstorms moving up through central Delaware, getting over to the southern tip of New Jersey at this hour. It's making slow progress so, a good bit of the afternoon around the tri-state will be dry, but as we get closer to the evening rush hour, the chance for rain will go up rather steadily, our high about eighty because of a lack of sun in most areas this afternoon, and then wet tonight with a low of seventy-two. The clouds will begin to break for some sun tomorrow, it'll be a warm and humid day, with a shower or thunderstorm in parts of the area, but overall it'll end up being a drier day with the high temperature tomorrow getting up to about, uh, eighty-four. Saturday, variable cloudiness and humid, another shower and thunderstorm or two around, the high eighty-four. Still unsettled on Sunday with some sunshine, the high eighty-six. Right now it's seventy-nine degrees in Teterboro and in West Hampton, seventy-seven and partly sunny in Central Park, relative humidity eighty-four percent, the wind northeast at six. Repeating the current temperature seventy-seven going up to eighty in midtown.

Oh, we are keeping tabs on the radar, and while nothing's cooking at this point in time, that rain that I was talking about out over, uh, parts of Delaware and parts of south Jersey, continues to creep slowly northward on up into, uh, Salem County at this point in time, not quite Ocean County. But while it's going to be mostly cloudy at this point in time for the next couple of hours with the high temperature of eighty-two degrees with some fog, we are going to pick up a period of rain and a thunderstorm or two very late this afternoon into tonight, with the low of seventy-two degrees. So yes, we will need the umbrella. Tomorrow turns, uh, partly sunny, but there's still going to be a shower or thunderstorm around, with the high of eighty-four degrees. Saturday turns yet more active with more numerous showers and thunderstorms, and a high of eighty-four. We won't dry it out completely until next week unfortunately. Right now it's eighty Caldwell, seventy-nine with the clouds Central Park, managing eighty-two in midtown.

Uh, we continue to not see any significant rainfall on our radar in the immediate tri-state area, but we are starting to see some thunderstorms developing, uh, in, uh, extreme southern New Jersey, there's actually one just south of Philadelphia, and other showers south of, uh, Cape May in the Atlantic Ocean are moving northward so, there will be showers and thunderstorms around the tri-state this afternoon and on into tonight. Uh, any of them can produce drenching downpours and local flooding, and that's the reason the flood watch remains in ef . . . in effect. Our high today will be in the low to middle-eighties, uh, low tonight in the low seventies. Partial sunshine for tomorrow, chance for a shower or thunderstorm, high about eighty-four and then, uh, partly sunny Wednesday, could be an afternoon thunderstorm, maybe it gets up to eighty-six or eighty-eight on Wednesday, and perhaps close to ninety for Thursday and Friday. Right now seventy-six and partly sunny in Central Park, temperature today going up to eighty-four.

There's going to be so much sun that the high pressure, both at the surface and aloft, is going to start to build. Now, we've been talking about that quite frequently during this, uh, very wet and humid pattern over the past two weeks. The high pressure has been, uh, located or positioned over the western Atlantic. Finally, now it's gonna overspread the landmass and that will contribute to some hot weather later on this week too. But first of all, some dense fog overnight, uh, it's already occurring at JFK where the visibility is one-sixteenth of a mile. Temperatures are going to remain in the mid-seventies tomorrow, a warm, humid day, high of about eighty-six, slight chance for a thunderstorm, and then Thursday and Friday, well, we'll be at least ninety and probably hitting, Friday, uh, ninety-two degrees, so get ready for the hot weather. Mostly cloudy, and seventy-five in midtown right now, the humidity ninety-four percent, the wind east three miles per hour, it's again mostly cloudy. Repeating the current temperature seventy-five, we're heading down to seventy-four.

The trend over the next few days around these parts is going to be for the sun to be out longer, for there to be less in the way of thunderstorm activity, and that means it's going to get warmer. Today will turn out at least partly sunny, and temperatures will get on up into the, uh, middle-eighties. Then it's partly cloudy tonight, with a low in the seventies. Hazy sunshine tomorrow and also Friday, with high temperatures around ninety, could even get into the nineties on Friday. And right now, Saturday also looks, uh, to be reasonably sunny, and the temperature still getting up to around ninety. Right now it is seventy-seven and partly sunny in Central Park, humidity ninety-three percent, and the wind is calm. Repeating the current temperature seventy-seven, going up to eighty-six today.

Partly cloudy, warm, humid conditions the rest of the night, low to mid-seventies, uh, come daybreak and hot, sticky weather coming up for the next, uh, few days with a good deal of sunshine. No mention of any precipitation until maybe Saturday afternoon or evening. There is going to be a front approaching from the north, and that may set off a thunderstorm, uh, afternoon temperatures, uh, right around ninety, ninety-two degrees each day. Currently we have eighty-six at LaGuardia, eighty-three degrees and partly cloudy in Central Park, a west wind at six. Repeating the current temperature eighty-three going down to seventy-four in midtown.

Well, it does appear that we have turned the spigot off and we've turned the thermostat up. Sunshine today with temperatures getting into the low, and even middle-nineties, and it'll be fair tonight with a low in the seventies. Hazy sunshine, hot again tomorrow, highs low to middle-nineties, and keep in mind that RealFeel temperature during the afternoon, uh, will be up into the upper-nineties, to even near triple digits. Saturday is still hot, there'll be some sun, high near ninety, but a cold front approaching by the end of the day could bring a thunderstorm, and then on Sunday there'll be less heat and less humidity. Right now it is seventy-seven and sunny in Central Park, humidity is eighty-one percent, wind from the northwest at three. Again the current temperature, seventy-seven going up to ninety-two.

Well, it's going to stay very warm and humid this afternoon, a combination of sunshine and building clouds, high temperatures around eighty-nine degrees. Those pop-up showers and thundershowers in northern New Jersey will become more widespread with time this afternoon and this evening. And there can be some flooding and downpours in a couple of spots late this afternoon into this evening, uh, due to the heating of the day, and also the approach of a cool front, which will be sweeping through the area tomorrow and later on tonight. Those thundershowers will carry on into the first part of tonight and again, it can be locally heavy and gusty. Still sticky later on tonight, lows around seventy-two. Tomorrow the transition, cooler, drier air mixing in, breaks of sunshine, just a brief shower in a couple of spots, high eighty-two. Monday partly to mostly sunny, the high near eighty, Tuesday and Wednesday mostly sunny, the high eighty-four, Wednesday's high eighty-six. Currently it's eighty-four, partly sunny in Central Park, the humidity seventy-one percent, the wind west at eight miles an hour. Repeating the current temperature eighty-four going up to eighty-nine.

Well, it'll be partly cloudy and will turn more comfortable overnight tonight as our dew points begin to lower, we'll have a low falling back to about sixty-four degrees. Lots of sunshine on Monday, pleasant temperatures, we'll see a high of eighty. On Monday night it'll be mostly clear, low-falling clouds, back to sixty-six in midtown, some of the suburbs dropping down to around sixty, very comfortable sleeping weather. Sunshine, a little bit warmer for Tuesday, with a high of eighty-four degrees. And looking ahead to Wednesday, plenty of sunshine, quite warm with a high of eighty-eight. Currently sixty-seven degrees at LaGuardia, sixty-six at Kennedy Airport, in Central Park, it's partly cloudy, sixty-five degrees, relative humidity one hundred percent, and we have a north wind at five miles per hour. Repeating the current temperature, sixty-five going down to sixty-four in midtown.

We've got a nice day coming up today with plenty of sunshine, temperatures this afternoon will top out at nearly the eighty degree mark, but the humidity will lower steadily and noticeably during the day. There's a slight chance for an afternoon thunderstorm east and north of, uh, most of the area, maybe north of the Tappan Zee Bridge, maybe parts of Connecticut, maybe the east end of Long Island, but most of us will, uh, not get any rain today, nor tomorrow, or Wednesday. Those days will be sunny and a high tomorrow in the middle-eighties, with the humidity still low. Upper-eighties on Wednesday, and then hazy sunshine, hot, and humid on Thursday, high near ninety. Right now it is sixty-eight and sunny in Central Park, temperature today going up to eighty.

Absolutely nothing that we have to worry about in terms of toting umbrellas around the region until the tail end of Friday so, with that being said, sunglasses between now and then. Eighty-six degrees this afternoon, a little cooler along the shore, clear sky tonight, seventy-two midtown, sixty-four suburbs. Now the humidity's been at a moderate level, yesterday, again today, it's at a high level tomorrow. Sunny to partly cloudy, high temperature eighty-eight degrees, and it gets even worse Thursday, with the aid of sunshine, we're in at ninety degrees, ditto that for Friday, although as I mentioned before, thunderstorms by day's end Friday. Right now seventy-nine Westhampton, eighty degrees with the aid of sunshine in Central Park, going up to a high of eighty-six in midtown.

Absolutely nothing cookin', at least as far as wet weather's going to be concerned, during the course of this afternoon, so with that, humidity's getting up there, and so is the temperature, eighty-nine degrees, but this ain't even the worst of the air mass. It's warm, it's humid tonight, no moisture. It's clear, seventy-four in midtown, sixty-eight degrees throughout the suburbs and if you're looking to broil, sunburn, bake, call it what you will, ninety-two degrees tomorrow, more sunshine. Now we are going to tone it down, uh, hazy sun, cloud mixture during the course of Friday, but it's still ninety-two degrees. A cool front that's due in toward the tail end of our Friday could trigger a thunderstorm, but I don't even think it's before the evening rush hour, I think we're looking at the time frame between eight o'clock and about two o'clock in the morning on Saturday. Right now it's eighty-four degrees at LaGuardia, and in Central Park with the aid of sunshine, we don't stop until we hit eighty-nine degrees in midtown.

Foggy conditions the rest of the night. We'll start the day with temperatures in the low to middle-seventies, climbing to the low nineties in the afternoon, with a lot of sunshine. Clear to partly cloudy, warm and sticky tomorrow night, seventy-six for an overnight low. Once again, low nineties before a cold front arrives on the scene, and it may touch off a late day or night-time thunderstorm. Behind that front we're looking at a nice weekend, not as hot Saturday, turning less humid during the day, partly sunny skies, about eighty-four degrees. Then a pleasant day Sunday, around eighty with lots of sunshine. Currently we have eighty-two at Teterboro, also in Central Park, a clear sky, a southwest wind at nine. Repeating the current temperature eighty-two going down to seventy-four in midtown.

OK, it's, uh, a wet one, damp, if you will, not soaking just yet, of course, I say that because where we're dealing with the heavy juices is right along the Mason-Dixon Line, and well in advance of it. A little bit of light rain, drizzle this afternoon, watch for the fog, high sixty-seven degrees. Low tonight sixty, eh, we continue with the damp stuff. But this heavy rain corridor along the Mason-Dixon Line that separates Pennsylvania and Maryland is going to be shifting northward very late tonight into tomorrow morning. Some of that heavy rain could try to, uh, skim the outer bridge crossing, and parts of Staten Island so, be cautious. Farther off to the north, light rain, drizzle tomorrow, with the high of sixty-nine. Now it warms to seventy-eight Thursday, but our latest cold front has another shower or thunderstorm, so we still need the umbrella. Right now sixty Caldwell, sixty-one with the clouds and drizzle in Central Park, going to sixty-seven degrees in midtown.

Well, September is "Be Kind to Writers and Editors Month" and individuals always have to worry about parts of speech and elements of style. We don't want, say, a writer to die a critical death. Today is renowned for cloudiness, but the big thing is, when will things improve? It's all predicated on the movement away of this moisture, and that's not going to happen today. We'll have periods of rain, some fog, high today sixty-nine, low tonight sixty-six. Tomorrow variable cloudiness, becoming warmer, remaining humid, a couple of showers are likely, a thunderstorm possible, high seventy-eight. But hear this preposition, partly sunny on Friday, high seventy-six, Saturday, partly to mostly sunny, high seventy-six. Not necessarily perfect, but good weather for vi . . . for visiting grammar's house. Currently sixty-three degrees in midtown, relative humidity ninety-six percent, winds out of the east at six, sixty-three heading for sixty-nine.

Well hang with me one more day and we're gonna get some much improved weather, but today, another day of clouds, another day of showers. There is, though, heavy rain immediately within the tri-state area, but there's a pretty good batch of thunderstorms in eastern Pennsylvania and so, uh, as we get through, uh, the late morning and into the afternoon, any of the showers or thunderstorms can produce some local flooding, downpours. Our high today seventy-eight, but the sun returns tomorrow, the humidity lowers, the high seventy-eight both days. The rest of the weekend will be sunny and nice, the highs in the middle-to-upper-seventies, and low humidity. Right now it's seventy-two and cloudy in Central Park, humidity one hundred percent, wind from the southwest at seven. Again the current temperature seventy-two going up to seventy-eight today.

Well, on Bermuda now, they're getting squalls and wind gusts to between fifty and sixty miles per hour, and as hurricane Fabian moves northward through, uh, the open Atlantic Ocean this weekend, it will cause some rough surf, and maybe some riptides on our beaches. But other than that, the weather will be just fine, a mix of sun and clouds tending toward the sunny side today, low humidity, and the high seventy-eight. Clear, cool tonight, low sixty-two in the city, fifties in the suburbs. Sunny and nice tomorrow, and Sunday with low humidity, the high tomorrow seventy-eight. Sunday's high eighty-two, and nice, uh, dry, sunny weather for the first couple of days of next week as well. Right now it is sixty-six and mostly sunny in Central Park, humidity seventy-four percent, wind from the north at seven. Repeating the current temperature, sixty-six going up to seventy-eight today.

High pressure is building to the northeast today, and it shoved all that rain off to our east. Looking at the current satellite picture, not a cloud in the sky this morning, it looks like a spectacular day, today's high about seventy-eight degrees. Clearing and cool tonight, low fifty-six in the suburbs, sixty-three in midtown. Plenty of sunshine once again for tomorrow, a warm afternoon with a high of eighty-two. We'll see a mix of clouds and sun on Monday, high seventy-eight. Partly to mostly sunny, breezy, and cooler for Tuesday and Wednesday, Wednesday's high about seventy-six. Currently it's sixty-one in Central Park, the relative humidity is eighty-one percent, the wind northwest at ten miles per hour. Repeating the current temperature, sixty-one going up to seventy-eight later today.

The weekend weather turned out to be every bit as nice as advertised, and the next couple of days will be just fine also, but we are watching moisture, uh, associated with remnants of tropical storm Henri, which are down along the Carolina coast, and if that moisture were to creep northward later in the week, our weather could go downhill, but for today and the next couple of days, it still looks pretty good. Sunny to partly cloudy today, high seventy-six, and fair tonight, low sixty-one. Mixed clouds and sunshine for tomorrow and Wednesday, high tomorrow seventy-two, Wednesday's high seventy-four, and right now partial sunshine on tap for Thursday, high seventy-six. So hopefully we're gonna be OK, at least for the next three to, maybe, four days. Right now sixty-seven and sunny in Central Park, humidity eighty-one percent, wind from the north at five. Again the current temperature sixty-seven going up to seventy-six today.

One high pressure area has departed, but a new one is developing to our north, and it looks like it'll strengthen and move southward and control the weather the next few days, meaning sunshine, a little bit of a cool breeze, going up to seventy-two today. Tonight clear, low sixty-one in midtown, fifty-four in many suburbs. And then for tomorrow and Thursday, sunshine, seventy-four tomorrow, seventy-six on Thursday, and Friday, partly sunny, high seventy-four. So some nice weather the next few days. Currently, winds out of the northeast at six miles per hour, the relative humidity eighty-two percent, sixty-four degrees is midtown, heading to seventy-two.

True artistry in the sky today, sunshine, occasional clouds, going up to seventy-six. Tonight, palatable, clear, low sixty-two in midtown to fifties in some suburbs. Tomorrow it'll be like it, easily, mostly sunny, high temperature seventy-eight. And Friday shouldn't have any poor traits, times of clouds and sunshine, a high of seventy-four degrees. On Saturday, uh, we may see some grays, mostly cloudy, windy, a chance for some rain, high seventy-two. Currently in midtown fifty-seven degrees, relative humidity ninety-three percent, wind out of the northeast at three miles per hour, fifty-seven heading to seventy-six with sunshine today.

Beautifully sunny day today, with a high pressure area in charge, it's going up seventy-eight this afternoon. Clear tonight, low fifty-six in some suburbs, sixty-four in midtown. Then tomorrow, sunshine will be followed by cloudiness, and the wind will start to increase in the afternoon. There's a storm off the Carolina coast, it hasn't moved anywhere in the last several days, but as the flow aloft becomes southerly, it probably will come off the coast, and that can mean some wind-driven rain at times on Saturday, with a high near seventy, and even Sunday is somewhat questionable, although the sky could start to clear in the afternoon, high eighty. Currently in midtown sixty-five degrees, relative humidity sixty-seven percent, winds out of the northeast at six miles per hour, and it's sunny, sixty-five heading for seventy-eight.

Huff and puff, that it does, but the wind is going to be relentless here, not just this afternoon, not just tonight, tomorrow, and to a certain extent, Sunday as well. So keep that in mind. Some sunshine followed by thickening clouds this afternoon, otherwise high seventy-two. It is dry, even this evening. We're gonna be A-OK, but the problem is the rain coming in a few hours after midnight, then it's off and on during the course of tomorrow. Uh, our storm system's going to be weakening in the rain department, I guess that's the good news, but when you factor in the wind, there's still going to be at least minor tidal flooding and beach erosion, high tomorrow at about seventy degrees. Sunday's partly sunny, more humid with the high of seventy-eight, but don't you just know that there could be a shower or a thunderstorm kicking around. Right now it's sixty-nine at LaGuardia, ditto Central Park, headed to seventy-two in midtown.

It's a cloudy day in New York City, and it looks like we're going to see the clouds, a little bit of rain and drizzle at times, just kind of a damp, cool afternoon with a gusty wind, and a high around seventy. It'll be cloudy and breezy tonight with occasional rain and drizzle, low of sixty-eight. Tomorrow mostly cloudy, humid, a couple of showers, could be a thunderstorm. Several dry hours tomorrow, though, a high of seventy-eight, and then for Monday, clouds will break for some sun at times, it'll be humid with a chance for a shower or thunderstorm, and a high of seventy-eight. Right now we have a, uh, sixty-eight degree reading at Morristown, seventy-one at Islip, cloudy and sixty-eight in Central Park, one hundred percent humidity, and a northeast wind at twelve.

We'll have patchy morning fog for the next couple of hours, otherwise a barely cloudy, humid day today with a few showers around, maybe an afternoon thunderstorm is possible, we'll have a high of seventy-eight. A couple more showers tonight, we'll fall back to about sixty-eight. Clouds, a little sunshine, muggy tomorrow, a coupla more showers, maybe a thunderstorm once again, high once again seventy-eight degrees. There's a small chance of a shower on Tuesday with clouds, some sunshine, high of seventy-eight. Clouds and sunshine, a dry day for Wednesday with a high of seventy-six. And all eyes turn to the south as we watch hurricane Isabelle, could be effecting our weather, come Thursday night, right into Friday. Currently in Central Park, a cloudy sky, seventy degrees, relative humidity one hundred percent, and a calm wind. Repeating the current temperature seventy going up to seventy-eight in midtown.

Isabelle is currently located a little over eleven hundred miles south, southeast of New York City, and moving west northwest at ten miles per hour. It's likely to hit somewhere in the Virginia, Maryland coastal area late this week. If it does that, then it's going to pass to our west, and we could have some gale-force, hurricane-force wind gusts, and very heavy rain as it does, but there's a more immediate threat going on right now. Flooding, rains, people had to be pulled from their cars, just west of Philadelphia, and also very heavy rain in northwest New Jersey from ongoing showers, and some of those locally heavy showers and thunderstorms will be around the area today and tonight. Then tomorrow it'll start to clear up and get beautiful, sunshine with afternoon temperatures in the seventies. And Wednesday and Thursday should be nice days until the storm approaches from the south, seventy-eight tomorrow, and seventy-six on Wednesday. Currently in midtown, seventy-three degrees, relative humidity ninety-three percent, winds out of the east at five miles per hour, seventy-three heading for seventy-eight.

It's a beautiful sunny day and it's going to stay that way, the humidity is lowering, and there's a nice, little, gentle, refreshing breeze, and the temperature today will get up close to eighty. And it's clear tonight with a low fifty-five to sixty and sunny tomorrow, high seventy-eight. Of course we are playing a waiting game, we're waiting to see what hurricane Isabelle is going to wind up doing and right now, it's weaker, considerably weaker, than it was yesterday, but still a formidable and dangerous storm, and it will probably cross northeast North Carolina on Thursday with winds in excess of one hundred miles per hour. Then it will weaken, but it can bring us a wind-swept, and perhaps heavy rain Thursday night, into part of

Friday. Right now it is sixty-five and sunny in Central Park, humidity eighty-four percent, wind from the northwest at six. Repeating the current temperature sixty-five going up to eighty.

We have some beautiful weather here, yet, for this afternoon and tonight. Things will start to deteriorate tomorrow, though, as hurricane Isabelle, uh, makes her landfall near, uh, Cape Hatteras, North Carolina, uh, pushing clouds, uh, into our sky, the wind picking up during the day tomorrow, temperatures will be in the low seventies. And then we will start to get into some rain later tomorrow night, and that'll be off and on into Friday, uh, some of that can be heavy and, uh, it'll be quite windy as well. But the main problem is going to be, uh, the piling up of the water along the eastern seaboard. Tides are going to be running well above normal, uh, perhaps, uh, three to five feet above normal, uh, causing coastal flooding, especially at times of high tide and that'll, uh, start later tomorrow night and, uh, right on through the day Friday. But by the weekend, the storm will move up into Eastern Canada and, in its wake, uh, actually some nice weather, lots of sunshine, temperatures will be in the middle-seventies Saturday and Sunday. Seventy-four and sunny in Central Park, with a northeast wind ten to twenty miles an hour. Repeating the current temperature seventy-four going up to seventy-eight in midtown.

The tropical storm warning that had been along the New Jersey coast is now been extended into parts of the city and adjacent counties, and that goes along with the forecast we've been talking about, a thirty-five mile per hour sustained wind, and gusts to fifty-five at the height of the storm, late tonight and tomorrow morning. The storm itself is just off the coast of North Carolina, heading straight into the northwest. It'll move up into central and western Virginia, western Pennsylvania, miss us by quite a bit, but it's a very big storm, and the gales extend out more than three-hundred miles from it. So for today, mostly cloudy, the wind slowly increasing, the high seventy-two. Then tonight and tomorrow, very windy, rain at times. At times, it'll be falling in horizontal sheets, it could be a thunderstorm, and peak winds should be sustained at thirty-five miles per hour for a while, with gusts of fifty-five. Low tonight sixty-six, high tomorrow seventy-two. Then for Saturday it's all gone, sunshine, some clouds, high seventy-eight degrees, and it looks like a nice rest of the weekend. Currently in midtown the wind out of the northeast at twelve, gusting to twenty-two miles per hour, relative humidity sixty-seven percent, sixty-six heading for seventy-two.

Well, for us, more a windstorm than a rain storm as, uh, Isabelle taken a track, uh, so far inland here, that most of the rain, uh, also shifting, uh, westward. Uh, we will see a little bit of rain here overnight and into tomorrow at times but, uh, that's probably not going to amount to a great deal. Uh, we are getting a very stiff wind, however, which is gusting past forty miles an hour, and that will continue right on through the night and, uh, finally through tomorrow morning, uh, start to diminish some, uh, tomorrow afternoon, uh, we could get some gusts as high as fifty, fifty-five miles an hour. Tides running two to three feet above normal, so coastal flooding may be our biggest headache. Uh, later tomorrow night, partly cloudy skies, diminishing winds, and then some nice weather for the weekend. Right now we have some light rain at LaGuardia, uh, we have seventy degrees at Central Park under a cloudy sky, with a northeast wind twenty gusting forty miles an hour. Repeating the current temperature seventy going down to sixty-four in midtown.

Well, Isabelle is in western Pennsylvania, moving rapidly northward and weakening very rapidly too, and the worst of the storm has already occurred here. There will still be gusty winds, uh, thirty to maybe forty miles per hour in gusts, and there'll still be a couple of, uh, squally showers around, but there will also be intervals of sunshine, and later in the day the breeze will subside. Tonight will be partly cloudy, our high today seventy-six, and the low tonight sixty-eight. Tomorrow a warm day, sunny to partly cloudy, up to eighty-four and mostly sunny Sunday, the high seventy-six. Right now it is seventy-three and cloudy in Central Park, humidity ninety-six percent, wind from the southeast, gusting to nineteen miles per hour. Again, the current temperature is seventy-three, going up to seventy-six today.

It'll be warm today with a mixture of clouds and sunshine, probably more sunshine in the afternoon hours, we'll have a high of eighty-two degrees. Clear to partly cloudy, comfortable tonight, low falling back to fifty-eight degrees in the suburbs, to sixty-four degrees in midtown. Lots of sunshine, a nice day tomorrow with a high of seventy-eight. On Monday, clouds will increase, we could see some showers late in the day, but more likely at night, with a high of seventy-four. And a chance of showers lingers into Tuesday, high on Tuesday seventy-two degrees. Currently seventy-two degrees at LaGuardia, sixty-eight at Newark, in Central Park a cloudy sky, seventy degrees, relative humidity eighty-four percent, and we have a calm wind. Repeating the current temperature seventy going up to eighty-two in midtown.

FALL

Well, we've got rain this morning and, in fact, it's going to really pour for several hours with the heaviest rain probably coming between, uh, eight to nine or about eleven o'clock. In that time period, there could be widespread street and highway flooding, so do allow yourself plenty of extra time to get around. It'll begin drying out late in the day, and tonight will become clear and cool. Tomorrow a sunny, beautiful day, afternoon high about seventy-two, and that ought to be the temperature in Central Park about three o'clock, as folks start gathering for the, uh, Dave Matthews concert. By nine o'clock, though, temperature down about probably to sixty-four. Thursday, sun followed by clouds, and there's a chance of showers again by the end of the day. Right now it is seventy and raining in Central Park, humidity one hundred percent, wind from the south, gusting to eighteen miles per hour. Again, the current temperature, seventy going up to seventy-six today.

A beautiful day, and, uh, sunshine will stay with us for the rest of the day, and temperatures get into the seventies this afternoon, very comfortable. For those folks, uh, who will be congregating in Central Park for the Dave Matthews concert tonight, about three o'clock, temperature at seventy-six, at six o'clock about seventy-two, by ten p.m. down to sixty-eight, and midnight, maybe down to sixty-four. So, cool after dark, maybe a light sweater or jacket. Tomorrow, sun followed by clouds, afternoon showers, and the high seventy-six. We get out, uh, toward Friday, it looks like a dry day with clouds and sun. Another chance of showers, though, long about Saturday. Sixty degrees and sunny now in Central Park, humidity seventy-two percent, and the wind light and variable. Again the current temperature sixty, going up to seventy-six today.

Uh, it is, eh, certainly a little warmer and more humid across the area during the course of this afternoon but, while we do have some sunshine, the clouds are going to be on the increase, and what we're dealing with over the Poconos, in terms of some wet weather, is going to continue to shift eastward. Now, once it gets east of the Delaware Water Gap, it is going to tend to, uh, thin out and weaken, but nonetheless I think, eh, during the middle, latter stages of this afternoon into early this evening there'll be a shower, thunderstorm in a couple of spots, high temperature seventy-six degrees, maybe a leftover shower tonight with the clouds, low sixty-two. Tomorrow, variably cloudy with this front stalling out, still can't rule out a shower, high seventy-four. But honestly, I think with the secondary storm system pulling down from the Great Lakes and the available moisture sitting on top of us, I'll look for steadier rain Saturday and a high of seventy-four. Right now it's seventy-two Caldwell, and in Central Park, that's with a lot of sunshine, mind you, going to seventy-six in midtown.

Our radar shows a smattering of showers immediately west and north of the city. Just about anybody can get a shower today, but the ones around this morning, uh, look like they're going, move away, and the chance of a shower this afternoon, this evening, is less than this morning. Even this morning they're just, uh, very spotty. It's going up to seventy-four today, down to sixty-four tonight. Tomorrow, uh, another, uh, case of a spotty shower possibility, but most of the day being OK, clouds, some sun, and humid, high seventy-six. Then rain is likely to fall in earnest tomorrow night into Sunday, followed by clearing later in the day Sunday, cooler with a high near seventy. Then for Monday, partly sunny and cool, high sixty-eight degrees. Currently in midtown it's sixty-three, the relative humidity eighty percent, it's mostly cloudy, watch for a couple of showers this morning, going up to seventy-four late today.

It's going to be a warm, sticky day today, with temperatures getting into the upper-seventies to near eighty degrees, with clouds and some intervals of sun, but also a couple of showers and even a thunderstorm will move through the area. There appears to be a thunderstorm right now on the radar, in the Hackensack area moving north about fifteen to twenty miles per hour. Then tonight, look for more rain and thunderstorms to move into the area, particularly later at night, and lasting into tomorrow morning, the overnight low sixty-six. We'll clear out late tomorrow as a cold front moves offshore, the high seventy-two, then cool air takes over for much of next week, temperatures Monday, Tuesday, and Wednesday only in the sixties with some sunshine each day. Right now across the tri-state, it is sixty-nine degrees in Somerville and in Westhampton, it's seventy-one and cloudy in Central Park, relative humidity one hundred percent, the winds southeast at eight miles an hour. Repeating the current temperature seventy-one going up to seventy-six in midtown.

Uh, we are looking at a clearing trend here tonight, eh, with temperatures comfortable, fifties, to around sixty, at daybreak. Cool weather much of the coming week and, uh, generally partly sunny skies each day, sixty-eight tomorrow, and sixty-four degrees for a high on Tuesday. Wednesday is the one day, eh, which, uh, may feature more clouds than sun, and it's the only day we're mentioning the possibility of seeing an afternoon or evening shower, high around sixty-four. And then Thursday, partly sunny, breezy, quite cool, only sixty-two. Currently we have . . . have, plenty of clouds, sixty-five degrees in Central Park, a northwest wind at ten to fifteen miles an hour. Repeating the current temperature sixty-five going down to sixty in midtown.

Showers now crossing parts of Brooklyn and Queens, will head out across the rest of Long Island and also western Connecticut during the next hour or two, they pretty well ended across northeast New Jersey, and they weren't that heavy to begin with. A few places, uh, came down hard enough to wet the ground, give one one-hundredth, or two one-hundredths of an inch, in any case, it turns out partly sunny for the afternoon, high sixty-eight. Clear tonight, low fifty-four in midtown, suburbs closer to fifty. Tomorrow partly sunny, breezy, and cool, high sixty-four. One o'clock for the first pitch for the Yankees, should be sixty-two degrees, partly sunny, our estimate. Wednesday, changing amounts of clouds and sunshine, maybe a shower, high sixty-four. Then Thursday, partly sunny, breezy, and quite cool, high fifty-nine. Currently in midtown fifty-nine degrees, relative humidity seventy-seven percent, wind out of the west at five, fifty-nine heading for sixty-eight.

The chilliest weather of this week actually still lies ahead of us, that chilliest moment will probably be Friday morning, in the meantime, today will be sunny to partly cloudy, with a high of sixty-six and at, uh, first pitch at Yankee Stadium this afternoon, it's probably around sixty-three and fair tonight, low fifty-four. Variable cloudiness tomorrow, there can be some sun, there could be a shower tomorrow, a high sixty-four, and then clouds and sun, brisk and quite cool for Thursday, the high fifty-nine. A mostly sunny day Friday, with a high of sixty-two. Right now it is fifty and sunny in Central Park, humidity is eighty-seven percent, wind from the west at three. Repeating the current temperature fifty going up to sixty-six today.

Well, partly cloudy skies, chilly conditions overnight, and we're looking at a windy, very cool day coming up tomorrow, with some sunshine, and a high temperature of only fifty-nine degrees, well below normal. Uh, the Yankees play tomorrow evening and, uh, looking at, uh, a partly cloudy sky, brisk conditions, and it's going to be a cool evening, temperatures, uh, at the start of the game around fifty-four degrees, and that temperature will continue to, uh, plunge tomorrow night under, uh, a clearing sky, uh, we'll get to around forty-six degrees in midtown, thirty-nine in some of the suburbs. Uh, Friday a good deal of sunshine, not as windy, as the high gets over to the East Coast, we'll still be upper-fifties for a high, and then some milder weather for the weekend, a little sunshine Saturday, a southwest breeze, and it'll be in the upper-sixties. The next front that may bring us a few showers, uh, later Saturday night and first thing Sunday morning. Currently fifty-six, mostly cloudy in Central Park, the west wind six to twelve miles an hour. Repeating the current temperature fifty-six going down to fifty in midtown.

A weak cold front is causing a couple of showers in northeast Pennsylvania right now, they're probably going to slide north of the city in about two or three hours, could reach places like Poughkeepsie, and then head into the Litchfield Hills, northwest Connecticut. Overall, a partly sunny day going to fifty-nine. For the Yankees, game two this evening, temperature dropping through the fifties, into the upper-forties, a chilly evening, it's going down to thirty-eight in some suburbs, forty-eight in midtown at daybreak. Tomorrow, sunshine for the most part, high fifty-nine, Saturday breezy, times of clouds and sun, but milder, going to sixty-eight. Next cold front will then approach, cause some showers Saturday night into Sunday, Sunday afternoon may start to clear, the high Sunday sixty-six. Currently the air is calm, relative humidity sixty-six percent, it's mostly sunny, fifty-two degrees heading for fifty-nine.

We start off with a chill in the air and frost in many of the outlying areas. Temperatures in the city got into the low forties, a few places got to the upper-thirties, but now with the dazzling sunshine and very little winds, it's going to be pretty comfortable this afternoon, as it goes up to fifty-nine. Fair and cold, uh, this evening, going down to forty-five to fifty, not as cold as last night, though. Then tomorrow, some sunshine followed by cloudiness, high sixty-four. A system now coming through Minnesota and Iowa could cause some showers tomorrow afternoon and tomorrow night, tomorrow night's low fifty-four. That system will whisk on out of here Sunday and it'll turn partly sunny, the high sixty-four, and Monday looks nice, partly sunny sixty degrees. So no real, uh, big weather problems the next few days. Currently in midtown forty-one degrees, relative humidity seventy-five percent, the air is virtually calm, sunny, going to fifty-nine.

Well, skies continue to cloud up as we have a cold front approaching from the west. It'll be windy and cooler the rest of today, and we will be . . . see a few periods of rain, from mid-morning on, a high of sixty-four. Nothing heavy in the rain, though, some clearing late tonight, it drops down to forty-four in the suburbs, and fifty-two in midtown. And, due to a cool Canadian air mass, it'll be brisk and cool tomorrow, Monday, and Tuesday, with partly to mostly sunny skies and highs in the upper-fifties to low sixties. It should begin to warm up nicely Wednesday, Thursday, and Friday. Right now it's sixty at JFK, fifty-eight at LaGuardia, mostly cloudy, fifty-seven in Central Park, sixty-nine percent humidity, a southwest wind at seven. Repeating the current temperature fifty-seven going up to sixty-four.

A very nice evening, uh, it's going to be cool overnight under a clear sky, low fifties in midtown, upper-forties in many of the suburbs at daybreak, and a warmer day coming up tomorrow, uh, with plenty of sunshine, a gentle breeze, uh, seventy-five in the afternoon. So some great weather for the, uh, start of the American League Championship series tomorrow night. Uh, the Yankees will have, uh, clear skies, light winds, temperatures will be in the upper-sixties when the game gets underway. Thursday, another nice day, mid-seventies, sunny to partly cloudy. Friday, uh, more clouds showing up, and that'll hold the temperature in the upper-sixties in the afternoon, then we could see some rain come in on Saturday. Currently we have sixty-two in Caldwell, sixty degrees, clear in Central Park, the winds south, eight to sixteen miles per hour. Repeating the current temperature sixty going down to fifty-three in midtown.

Well, we're looking at, uh, clear, mild weather conditions tonight, only dropping to around sixty degrees in, uh, midtown at daybreak. Uh, patchy fog will be around for the early morning hours, and then it'll be turning mostly sunny, uh, as the day wears on. A warm afternoon, seventy-six for a high temperature, uh, again, very pleasant weather for game two tomorrow evening, temperature will be around seventy degrees as the game gets underway and, uh, it will be mild tomorrow night, a low around sixty-two. Friday may also have some fog early, otherwise clouds, some sunshine, at around sixty-eight. Over the weekend, the wind picking up Saturday, mostly cloudy, we'll start the rain either late in the day, or more likely, Saturday night and that'll likely continue right on through Sunday. We have sixty-seven degrees, a clear sky in Central Park, a southwest wind at eight. Repeating the current temperature sixty-seven going down to sixty in midtown.

Uh, we're going to have a nice day today with plenty of sunshine, and temperatures warm into the seventies, although a little cooler right at the shore. At Yankee Stadium this evening, it should be close to seventy at first pitch, or at least the upper-sixties, and stay in the sixties throughout the game, so another very comfortable October evening for baseball. Tomorrow a mix of clouds and sun, back up into the seventies. We're going to continue to watch, for the next couple of days, this moisture that's down across the Carolinas. It's not racing northward, but there are some signs that at least some of it will come northward, and there is a chance for rain here by the end of the day on Saturday. Right now fifty-nine and sunny in Central Park, humidity is eighty-nine percent and the wind is calm. Again, the current temperature, fifty-nine going up to seventy-six today.

We do have low clouds this morning and, uh, a few fog patches but, uh, we think they'll evaporate as we get to mid-to-late morning, and there will be several hours of sun during the middle of the day, this afternoon, we'll get temperatures into the seventies. Then it's partly cloudy tonight, low sixty-two. Partly sunny, breezy tomorrow, high seventy to seventy-four, and then on Sunday, we're going to have to deal with a combination of a cold front approaching from the west and, uh, low pressure, uh, down along the Carolina coast that probably brings us clouds Sunday. There is at least a chance for some rain. Then the sun's back on Monday for Columbus Day, with a high of sixty-eight. Right now it's sixty-one and cloudy in Central Park, humidity ninety-three percent, wind from the northeast at ten. Repeating the current temperature sixty-one going up to seventy-four today.

And we are going to end up with plenty of fog, well, decent weather, as we hook through the rest of the afternoon, quite honestly. What a beautiful afternoon, temperatures heading to about seventy in the Park, plenty of sunshine throughout the tri-state area. We are going to see clouds unfortunately increase as we go through the night, though, and there is actually the possibility for a little drizzle later tonight and the early part of tomorrow, areas of fog, as well, as we start tomorrow morning, clouds might actually be breaking as early as later tomorrow. We are going to hit about sixty-eight tomorrow, seventy-two Monday with plenty of sun, and we are going to end up with beautiful weather again Tuesday, cool, sixty-eight degrees, but we should have plenty of sunshine. Seventy-one at Newark, seventy at JFK, same thing in the Park. It's mostly sunny in New York, relative humidity fifty-nine percent, wind northeast at twelve miles an hour, gusting to eighteen miles an hour, seventy now, we'll drop to sixty overnight in midtown.

Oh, we're looking at partly cloudy skies here this evening. Overnight it'll be mainly clear, breezy, temperatures will be in the low to mid-fifties for the morning rush hour. Uh, a beautiful day coming up tomorrow with, uh, sunshine and, uh, unseasonably warm conditions, uh, temperatures be in the low seventies in the afternoon. Uh, clear tomorrow night, low fifties and upper-forties, and Tuesday, sunshine will be giving way to clouds, uh, ahead of the next, uh, frontal system, a high around sixty-six. That next front is likely to generate some steady rain, uh, it'll start late in the day or Tuesday evening, and continue through much of the night, uh, it'll end early Wednesday, and the rest of the day it's going to be quite windy behind this system, clouds, some sunshine with a high around sixty-four. Currently seventy-two degrees in Newark, we have sixty-eight in Central Park, clouds, some sun, a north wind, ten to twenty miles an hour. Repeating the current temperature sixty-eight going down to fifty-six in midtown.

Today will be dry, we'll have variable cloudiness, not out of the question if a shower shows up this afternoon, but overall a dry day, moderate temperature going to sixty-six. Not a lot of wind, either, and there'll be some sunshine, there's some now. Then rain will move in tonight, we have cloudiness during the next few hours. There can be some sunny breaks as a little slot of dry air comes in, and then the clouds will thicken overhead, and we do expect some rain to be around later this afternoon and this evening, today's high fifty-eight, going down to forty-five tonight. Then tomorrow, partly sunny, breezy, and cool, high fifty-six and, at first pitch time for game one of the World Series, temperature fifty-two degrees and partly clear. Sunday partly sunny, high sixty-two, Monday mostly sunny and sixty-two. Currently in midtown it's fifty-two, the relative humidity is sixty percent, the air is virtually calm. It's mostly cloudy, heading to fifty-eight today.

The rain that we had overnight is long gone. The radar is all quiet now, and we'll see enough sunshine today to boost temperatures well into the fifties this afternoon. If you're heading to The Bronx for game one of the World Series, dress warmly, it'll be dry, partly cloudy, fifty-two at the first pitch. Partly to mostly cloudy overnight, down to forty-eight in midtown, and forty-two in the colder suburbs. Gotta watch out for a weak area of low pressure to move by the area late tonight and tomorrow morning, there may be a little rain in the area with it, and clouds will break for some sun later tomorrow, with a cool breeze, and a high close to sixty. More sunshine than clouds Monday, high sixty-two, but the rain may return Tuesday afternoon with the high of sixty-six. Currently forty-three in Belmar and in Islip, forty-five and cloudy in Central Park, relative humidity one hundred percent, the wind west at six miles per hour. Repeating the current temperature forty-five going up to fifty-eight in midtown.

Well, we are looking at a shower in one or two spots, as we head through the early part of the afternoon, but probably after two or three in the afternoon, that chance of a shower will be diminishing to all but nothing. A little bit of sunshine, a high of sixty degrees, but skies will clear on out for game two of the World Series, temperature fifty-four degrees for first pitch, mainly clear tonight, low forty-four. Sunshine, some clouds on Monday, the high sixty. It'll be windy on Tuesday, maybe some showers possible, the high sixty-six. Cloudy to partly sunny, windy and cooler Wednesday, high fifty-eight. Fifty degrees and cloudy in Central Park, humidity coming in at eighty-nine percent, wind variable at six miles an hour. Repeating the current temperature fifty, we're going up to sixty in midtown.

Sunny to partly cloudy for the entire day, it's going up to sixty. Partly cloudy tonight, not as cold as last night, low fifty-two. Tomorrow we have a shot at seventy degrees, it'll be a windy day, though, variable cloudiness, could be a couple of showers as a cold front approaches, probably won't rain very long, if it rains at all. Then Wednesday, behind the cold front, windy and cooler with clouds and sun, perhaps a brief shower, high fifty-six. Thursday, partly sunny still windy and cool, high fifty-four. No major storms coming this week. Currently in midtown forty-six degrees, the relative humidity is seventy-three percent, and the air is virtually calm, forty-six heading for sixty.

Well, partly cloudy, breezy overnight, we'll be in the low fifties at daybreak, and temperatures tomorrow staying in the fifties, uh, gusty northwest wind, clouds, a little bit of sun, it may even shower. Tomorrow night, uh, we'll get chilly, uh, around forty degrees in midtown, upper-thirties in many of the suburbs. Thursday a chilly day, clouds, some sun, brisk, uh, with about, uh, temperatures in the upper-forties. And then as we get toward the end of the week, uh, high pressure, which will be dropping in from central Canada, gets over to the eastern seaboard, we'll see more of the sun, temperatures in the mid-fifties on Friday, and then back into the middle-sixties on Saturday. Currently we have sixty under a cloudy sky in Central Park, wind out of the north at ten to eighteen miles per hour. Repeating the current temperature sixty going down to fifty-four in midtown.

Uh, mostly cloudy, brisk, cold overnight, eh, a sprinkle here and there, but nothing of consequence. Temperatures will be in the upper-thirties at daybreak, we'll climb to forty-nine in the afternoon, clouds, breaks of sun, it still may shower. Uh, we'll drop back into the thirties tomorrow night, and then a warming trend Friday through the weekend, as the big high gets over to the East Coast, and the wind goes back around to the south, uh, a lot of sunshine. We'll be in the middle-fifties on Friday, low sixty Saturday, mid-sixties on Sunday under a partly sunny sky. In Central Park right now, forty-one degrees under a cloudy sky, with a north wind at ten. Repeating the current temperature forty-one going down to thirty-nine in midtown.

No wet weather around these parts per our live scan radar, but it is partly sunny, it is windy, and it is colder than any day in recent memory, high temperature just forty-nine, factor in that wind, the RealFeel temperature, believe it or not, this hour is thirty-nine. That's cold! As a matter of fact, it's going to be clear and cold tonight, thirty-seven midtown, thirty-two suburbs. While that's happening, in the seventies in Miami, all game long. Good weather, at least down in that part of our nation. Meanwhile, we'll have sunshine, a little cloud cover tomorrow, not as cold, high fifty-four. Partly sunny Saturday, high sixty degrees, more clouds Sunday, with a high of sixty-six. We probably won't get wet until sometime on Monday. Right now forty-four Bridgeport, and in Central Park we've toned it down to partly sunny, but we'll manage a high of forty-nine this afternoon in midtown, high sixty-two.

It's bright and brimming with sunshine, and it will go up to fifty-two this afternoon. Tonight, another chilly one, frosty, thirty-four in some suburbs, to forty-four in midtown. Tomorrow, sunshine mixing with clouds, but it's suddenly going to get a little milder, going to fifty-eight. And Sunday is apt to turn cloudy, it could rain later in the day, high sixty-six. Monday, cloudy and windy with rain likely, high sixty-two. So, obviously tomorrow would be better of the two days for outdoor activities. Currently thirty-seven degrees in midtown, relative humidity sixty-nine percent, winds out of the north at five miles per hour, thirty-seven heading to fifty-two.

Well, we've got a nice bright and sunny morning, and it looks like the dry weather will hold on through game six of the World Series tonight. We could have the first pitch temperature of fifty-four, but during the day today, it's going to be nice. It'll go up to about fifty-eight this afternoon, could be a little drizzle after midnight tonight, a low of forty-eight in the suburbs, and fifty-two in midtown. Cloudy, breezy on Sunday, just a little rain and drizzle at times, a high of sixty-four, and a soaking rain and wind for Sunday night and Monday, the high Monday about sixty-two. Right now, thirty-seven at JFK, it's forty-four at LaGuardia, we have sunshine, forty-five in Central Park, sixty-three percent humidity, and a southeast wind at six, forty-five right now headed up to fifty-eight today.

Well, it'll be mostly cloudy and milder today, we'll have a shower in spots, also some patchy drizzle, a couple of light showers moving across portions of western Suffolk County, as we speak. We'll have a high today of sixty-seven degrees. Mostly cloudy, breezy tonight, a bit of rain possible, with a low falling back to fifty-eight. Real rain comes in tomorrow, windy with wind-swept rain, could even be a thunderstorm, some of that rain heavy at times, with a high of sixty-five. Dry again on Tuesday, clouds and sunshine, with a high of fifty-eight. Maybe a little rain to start Wednesday, breezy, with clouds breaking for some sunshine, with a high right around sixty. Currently sixty-three deg . . . degrees in Caldwell, in Central Park it's sixty-four, relative humidity ninety percent, and a variable wind at seven miles per hour. Repeating the current temperature sixty-four going up to sixty-seven in midtown.

We had a squall line associated with a cold front, uh, which went through the, uh, region, during the, uh, late afternoon hours, uh, some places causing, uh, fifty, sixty mile-an-hour wind gusts, uh, but like I said, that has pushed well off to our east, uh, the rain is just about over as well. The radar is showing us dried out across northwestern New Jersey, down to about Philadelphia, and it'll be coming to an end in the city over the next hour or so, and, uh, continue to end from west to east, then out Long Island. Overnight, partial clearing, a low of fifty degrees. And tomorrow is a nice day, sixty under a partly sunny sky, could see a little rain once again late tomorrow night and Wednesday morning, but this'll be light, and then clearing Wednesday afternoon, the high of sixty-two. Fifty-six degrees and light rain in Central Park with a southwest wind, eight to sixteen miles per hour. Repeating the current temperature fifty-six going down to fifty in midtown.

And it's a nice day, uh, and we've got a break in the rain today, with sunshine followed by increasing clouds, temperatures get up to around sixty, but the combination of a new storm over the Great Lakes, and moisture along the Carolina Coast, will combine to bring us rain beginning late tonight. It will rain through tomorrow morning, and end tomorrow afternoon, and some of that rain will be heavy enough to cause street and highway flooding. Tomorrow morning's rush hour is likely to be very messy, so plan on allowing yourself some extra time. Sunshine back for Thursday, though, Friday and Saturday also look like sunny days, with high temperatures around seventy. Right now it's forty-eight and sunny in Central Park, humidity seventy-three percent, the wind is calm. Again, the current temperature, forty-eight, going up to sixty today.

As we continue to keep tabs on our, uh, live scan radar, the, uh, steadiest, heaviest of the rain is already east of Islip. That's going to be moving away within the, uh, next hour here. Farther off to the west of that, ur, rain corridor, honestly to just, you know, light rain showers, sprinkles if you will. Now, there are additional showers back over Pennsylvania, but they're hit or miss. So, you know, we're still going to get on the wet side this afternoon, but it's nothing compared to what we just went through. Otherwise, rather cloudy, high temperature this afternoon fifty-nine degrees. We clear it tonight, forty suburbs, forty-eight midtown. And the sun is back! It's beautiful! I say that because it's sixty-four tomorrow, sixty-eight Friday, seventy degrees on Saturday. I hope you have outdoor plans after this mess we're going through now. Fifty-six this hour Caldwell and in Central Park, we'll manage fifty-nine this afternoon in midtown.

Gorgeous weather continuing across the region and, the beauty of the air mass, and I passed this along before, but I want to do so again, if you don't have opportunity to take advantage of it this afternoon or perhaps tomorrow, it's still gonna be great, Saturday, Sunday, and there's no threat of wet weather until next week. So, with that being said, sixty-four this afternoon, mainly clear tonight, forty-two suburbs, fifty-two midtown. Sunny to partly cloudy tomorrow, breezy, high sixty-eight. Partly sunny on Saturday, with a high of seventy-two degrees. If there's a stumbling block, could be a little of morning fog tomorrow or Saturday, but I wouldn't count on it. Count on fifty-nine degrees this hour in Bridgeport, sixty-one Belmar, fifty-nine, by the way, with the sun in Central Park, going to sixty-four in midtown.

It is going to be beautiful today, high temperature sixty-eight with the sunshine. We do have bad news for one Halloween monster, however, who likes to fly it's kite in a thunderstorm, the Franklinstein. Anyway, partly cloudy tonight, going down to fifty-eight. Intervals of clouds and sunshine tomorrow, breezy and warm, high seventy-four. For the marathon Sunday, partly sunny, high sixty-four. Monday, breezy and very warm for early November, with clouds and sun, perhaps a shower, high seventy-six, and then probably cooler on Tuesday. But for today, going to sixty-eight. Currently fifty-two degrees in midtown, relative humidity eighty-seven percent, the air is calm and it's sunny, fifty-two heading to sixty-eight.

Well, I don't think you should sit around the house today, enjoy this Indian summer weather. We're going to have temperatures go up to seventy-four for this first day in November. How about that? Normal high is fifty-nine. Partly to mostly cloudy, a couple of sprinkles tonight, down to fifty-four. Tomorrow cooler, but still very nice, clouds and sun, a high of sixty-four. And for Monday, sun and clouds, record-challenging warmth, now, we're expecting a high of seventy-six. The record is seventy-eight set in 1990. We'll be very close to that. Right now fifty-four at White Plains, it's fifty-three at Bridgeport. Very mild morning, cloudy, fifty-seven in Central Park, eighty-three percent humidity, a southwest wind at six. Repeating the current temperature fifty-seven headed up to seventy-four.

Checking the current radar, we see a couple of showers cruising through the Long Island Sound, also a couple of showers about to, uh, move across, uh, Staten Island at this time, a hit or miss shower out there this evening. Later on tonight, partly to mostly cloudy, the low fifty-eight. Record-challenging warmth tomorrow, intervals of clouds and sunshine, the high seventy-six. The record is seventy-eight set back in 1990. Maybe a few fog patches tomorrow night, perhaps a shower later on, low fifty-eight. A flow from the ocean sets up Tuesday and Wednesday, inland areas can still climb into the seventies on Tuesday. We should see a high around sixty-four in New York City, variable clouds, and a chance of that shower. A better chance with more generous rainfall here on Wednesday, the high sixty-four. Thursday, a shower possible early, then mostly cloudy, high sixty. Currently it's sixty-four, mostly cloudy in Central Park, the relative humidity seventy-two percent, the winds south to southwest, averaging five to ten miles an hour. Repeating the current temperature sixty-four going down to fifty-eight.

Reasonably warm day coming up today, in fact, so unseasonably warm that we may challenge record-high temperatures. That record-high in Central Park is seventy-eight, goes back to 1990 and, uh, that's certainly a number that's reachable. Some fog outside of the city this morning, otherwise just kind of a murky start to what will be, at least, a partly sunny day, then clouds tonight and, uh, the low fifty-eight. Tomorrow, clouds and cooler, and there may be a shower, high tomorrow sixty in midtown, sixty-five in adjacent New Jersey, but only fifty-five on, uh, Long Island and in Connecticut. Chance of showers Wednesday, maybe into Thursday morning, and then partly sunny Thursday afternoon, the high around sixty. Right now it is sixty-three and partly cloudy in Central Park, humidity is ninety-three percent, wind from the southwest at ten. Again, the current temperature sixty-three, going up to seventy-six today.

A tricky day of weather today, uh, clouds and sun will probably alternate, uh, but the thing is it's a lot cooler than yesterday when we got to a record high of seventy-nine. Today the temperature can sneak into the sixties for a while this morning, then wind up in the fifties again this afternoon and, uh, drizzle and fog settling in this evening, and remaining with us into tomorrow morning. Tomorrow gets milder, temporarily, up to sixty-eight, and then we get some rain tomorrow night into Thursday morning. Clearing beginning later Thursday, followed by a partly sunny, windy, cool day Friday, high fifty-six. Right now the weekend looks dry, but chilly. Right now it is mostly sunny and fifty-nine in Central Park, humidity ninety-six percent, wind has shifted into the northeast now at seven. Again, the current temperature fifty-nine, going up maybe to sixty-six this morning, dropping again during the afternoon.

Ah, take your umbrella, uh, take your coat, uh, leave your sunglasses behind today, they would certainly be excess baggage. It'll be overcast, drizzle, rain at times, uh, areas of fog, and that's the case today and tonight. It will slowly get milder, but this high of sixty-eight that we're talking about today probably does not occur until after dark, until some time between eight p.m. and midnight, and most of the day today will be considerably cooler than that. Cloudy tomorrow, some rain in the morning, sun's back for Friday but cool, high fifty-six.

Sunshine both days of the weekend, but cold with highs in the forties. Right now fifty-one and cloudy in Central Park, humidity ninety-six percent, wind from the northeast at ten. Again, the current temperature fifty-one going up to sixty-eight, but not until the evening.

We'll have cloudiness this morning, uh, not much going on rainfall-wise the next several hours, but rain will fall this afternoon and this evening, and we can get a soaking at that time, the high today sixty-two. Tonight, cloudy and cooler, low forty-six. Tomorrow brisk and cool, times of clouds and sunshine, high fifty-eight, and then a chilly, but dry weekend. Saturday sunny, high forty-six, Sunday sunny, high forty-six, not quite as chilly early next week. Currently in midtown fifty-eight degrees, relative humidity ninety-three percent, wind north at six miles per hour, fifty-eight heading to sixty-two.

Partly to mostly sunny today, it's going up to sixty. Clearing tonight, low thirty-two in some suburbs, forty in midtown. Tomorrow much colder than today, with some sunshine and a brisk wind, high forty-six, then we have the total lunar eclipse tomorrow night. It's totally the opposite of the case of solar eclipses, where total eye protection is necessary, whether the eclipse is partial or total. In this case you don't need any eye protection, it's a total one this time not a partial. Sunday, brisk and still cold, high forty-six. Monday, some sunshine followed by increasing cloudiness, high fifty-four. Currently, winds out of the north at six miles per hour, the relative humidity eighty-six percent, forty-nine degrees in midtown heading to sixty.

It's going to be a chilly day today, no no no no eg . . . uh, way to get around it. Temperatures have been falling all morning long, we'll only recover to about, let's say forty-six, for a high this afternoon in midtown, despite a lot of sunshine. And it looks like a freeze-morning for tonight, late tonight, between midnight and eight a.m., when it'll be clear, breezy, and cold, lows in the twenties in most suburbs, thirty-two in midtown. Sunny tomorrow, brisk and cold, high forty-four. Sunny to partly cloudy Monday, high fifty-two, the clouds return Tuesday with them, a chance for some rain on Veteran's Day, the high fifty-four. Right now it's thirty-nine in Caldwell and White Plains, forty-one and sunny in Central Park, relative humidity forty-six percent, the wind northwest at nine, gusting to twenty-one miles an hour. Repeating the current temperature forty-one going up to forty-six in midtown.

A kind of a good and bad thing today. We have a lot of sunshine out there today, that's a good thing, but it's going to be very chilly out there, brisk as well, we'll have a high of only forty-four degrees. Clear and cold again tonight, low falling back to about thirty-four degrees in midtown, a lot of the suburbs falling back into the twenties, though. Mostly sunny, still a bit chilly tomorrow, with a high up to about fifty degrees. Now to look ahead to Tuesday and Wednesday, mostly cloudy skies, could be some rain or drizzle, either day, Tuesday's high fifty-two, Wednesday's high up to fifty-six. Currently thirty-four degrees in White Plains, thirty-four degrees in Teterboro, in Central Park, lots of sunshine, thirty-three, relative humidity forty-seven percent, and a northwest wind at five miles per hour. Repeating the current temperature thirty-three going up to forty-four in midtown.

It is chilly, but it's going to warm up to fifty this afternoon, that's not all that warm, but it won't be very windy. Clear early tonight, partly cloudy after midnight, low thirty-four in some suburbs to forty-one in midtown. Now, tomorrow will be a little warmer than today, going to fifty-four, but the breeze is going to be a little stronger and clouds will increase, could be a little bit of rain in the afternoon and at night, as a warm front approaches. Wednesday the warm front will go by, but a cold front will approach. That could mean some rain, high fifty-eight. Then behind the cold front, times of clouds and sunshine, blustery, chilly again Thursday, high fifty-two. Currently thirty-four, relative humidity fifty-eight percent, the air is virtually calm, it's sunny, thirty-four heading for fifty.

It's a little warmer this morning than it was at this time yesterday. Cloudiness will increase today, could be a little rain or drizzle later this afternoon, going up to fifty-two, only down to fifty tonight. Now, tomorrow will feel genuinely mild, there will be a fair amount of cloudiness around, maybe a shower, but most of the time just the clouds, high sixty. Then a strong cold front will sweep through tomorrow night, or first thing Thursday, triggering some gusty showers behind it. Winds could gust to forty miles an hour out of the northwest Thursday as temperatures drop from the fifties into the forties. Friday, sunny but with a cold wind, high forty-six, so we'll be back in the same place we started the week. Currently in midtown forty-one degrees, relative humidity fifty-seven percent, winds southwest at three miles per hour, it's mostly cloudy, forty-one heading for fifty-two.

Well, while the clouds continue to hang tough across the region here this afternoon, high temperature fifty-eight degrees, we are going to see some holes, uh, developing here but, I tell you what, the . . . very easily it turns out overcast later tonight, rain is in after midnight, could even be a heavy, gusty thunderstorm by daybreak, with a low temperature of fifty degrees. Tomorrow, dry and it's going to turn out partly sunny, but there's problems, it's going to be the wind, upwards of fifty miles an hour on occasion, speed restrictions. So that's going to equal more delays than we typically have for the morning rush hour. High tomorrow morning fifty-two, temperatures into the forties during the afternoon, and winds will continue to be just as strong tomorrow night, maybe coming down a notch on Friday, but still windy enough with some sun, the chance of a snow flurry, Friday's high forty-four. Right now fifty-five in Teterboro, also in Central Park, going to fifty-eight in midtown.

We're going to have very strong winds today. The winds are going to gust past fifty miles per hour at times and this is going to bring down some tr . . . tree limbs, power lines. Already thousands of people as close as Philadelphia are without power, across parts of New Jersey as well. This all spreading north-eastward. The other thing today is the temperature's going to be falling, so dress warmly. It's going to be going down through the forties, could even reach the upper-thirties by seven o'clock this evening. There could be a snow flurry or two, overall though, a dry pattern. And then tonight, the temperature is going to be sinking toward thirty-three, thirty-four degrees, as a strong wind continues. Tomorrow a little less wind, the high forty-four, but it'll feel like it's freezing with the RealFeel temperature. Saturday, sunshine, high fifty-two, Sunday partly to mostly sunny, high fifty-two degrees. But today the main story is the wind, and currently the wind is out of the west, northwest at twelve, gusting to twenty-eight miles per hour, a few communities have gusts over forty. The temperature, sixty degrees, heading down into the fifties and then the forties.

We're still getting winds gusting in the, er, forty, forty-five mile per hour range. We don't expect them to be as fierce as yesterday, but they're certainly still formidable and it will, by all counts, still be a windy day, uh, it will also generally be a sunny day, with temperatures getting into the forties. And tonight clear, diminishing wind, with lows in the thirties. Less wind tomorrow, it should be a pretty good day tomorrow, sun, followed by some clouds, the high fifty-two, and then mostly cloudy Sunday, high also fifty-two. Not a . . . out of the realm of possibility that there's a little bit of rain around on Sunday as well. Right now partly cloudy, thirty-five in Central Park, humidity forty-two percent, wind from the west, gusting to twenty-four. Again the current temperature thirty-five going up to forty-four.

Well, you know it's a pretty nice morning out there, we have plenty of sunshine and unfortunately we can't shake that, uh, chilly, gusty breeze. It won't be as windy as the last couple of days, but nonetheless the chilly, gusty breezes continue for one more afternoon, along with the sunshine, a high of around fifty-two, that's pretty much typical for this time of year. Partly to mostly cloudy tonight, uh, low forty-two. Tomorrow we'll call it variably cloudy, we'll see some sun at times, the high around fifty-two. Then times of sun and clouds and, uh, about fifty-two on Monday, so not much change through Monday, and then a chance for rain coming in on Tuesday.

Well, it's going to be a mostly cloudy day today, we could see a couple of sprinkles around for about the next hour or two. Other than that, it looks mainly dry and just cloudy, with a high of fifty degrees. Mostly cloudy tonight, a little more rain and drizzle comes in after midnight, with the low slipping back to about forty-four. Maybe a little rain, drizzle to start the day tomorrow, then some afternoon sunshine with a high of fifty-two. Mostly cloudy day on Tuesday, chance of rain, especially during the afternoon and the nighttime hours, with a high of fifty-six. As we look ahead to Wednesday, a cloudy, windy day with periods of rain. A little bit warmer, though, with a high around sixty. Currently in Central Park, we have a cloudy sky, it's forty-five degrees, relative humidity sixty percent, and a wind out of the west at five miles per hour. Repeating the current temperature forty-five going up to fifty in midtown.

Partly to mostly cloudy tonight, patchy fog, temperatures not moving much. We'll still be in the forties for the morning rush hour, and then tomorrow, a mostly cloudy day, maybe a bit of drizzle in the afternoon with a high of fifty-four. Mostly mild weather for the rest of the week, but it's certainly going to turn very, very wet as well. Uh, we have a front right now which is cutting down through the Plains and into Texas, uh, it's going to be pushing over to the East Coast, stalling here, as a storm forms on the boundary, and brings us quite a dose of rain from Wednesday onward, uh, especially, uh, Wednesday afternoon and night, it could be heavy at times, a high of fifty-eight. Thursday and Friday, cloudy, windy, additional rain, uh, a good, uh, likelihood, a high temperature both days of fifty-four. We have forty-eight degrees right now in Central Park, it's a cloudy sky, northeast wind at seven. Repeating the current temperature forty-eight going down to forty-six in midtown.

We have a lot of cloudiness, but there won't be much production from these clouds because they're really not all that thick, even though it looks gray, the high temperature this afternoon about fifty to fifty-four degrees. It may just hold up like yesterday, it got to fifty in the late morning, then just sat there. Certainly, it's not going to be all that warm today, cloudy and breezy tonight, whatever it gets to today, it doesn't drop much tonight, the low fifty. Then tomorrow cloudy, windy, becoming warmer than today, warmer for November, of course, a bit of rain early, steadier, and heavier in the afternoon, high sixty-two. Thursday, cloudy and windy with periods of rain, high fifty-four, and Friday also could be damp, with a high of fifty-four. Currently it's forty-six, the relative humidity ninety-three percent, wind light and variable, it's forty-six heading to fifty-four.

It isn't raining everywhere but where it is raining, the showers are heavy, and a batch of them are crossing the area, from southwest to northeast right now. The main batch of rain is going to be later this afternoon and this evening, it's almost like a wall of water on the radar and will actually appear that way, but it'll be pouring late this afternoon and this evening, we can even get a thunderstorm at that point, temperatures reaching the low sixties. Then tonight the rain'll taper off late, and tomorrow, come to an end for a while. Now the big question for tomorrow and Friday, is whether we actually get additional rainfall or it shifts offshore. It's going to be a very close call, and we can be expecting temperatures in the mid-fifties. The weekend looks good, partly sunny Saturday, high sixty degrees. Currently in midtown fifty-seven, relative humidity one hundred percent, wind out of the south at nine, fifty-seven heading to sixty-one.

Our radar shows that there is still some more rain for us this morning, especially from the city across Long Island into Connecticut, much less across New Jersey, just a few left-over showers are starting to clear, back of the Delaware River. That whole trend will progress eastward, and we'll see some clouds breaking for sunshine later today, the high fifty-six. Clear and chilly tonight, low thirty-six in some suburbs, forty-six midtown. Tomorrow a beautiful sunny day, high fifty-eight, and the weekend, spectacular for the week before Thanksgiving, sunshine, high both days sixty degrees. Currently, the winds out of the north at four miles per hour, relative humidity ninety-two percent, forty-six degrees in midtown heading to fifty-six this afternoon.

It's a fine morning, we'll have dazzling sunshine today, becoming milder, high temperature sixty-two. Clear tonight, low forty in some suburbs, to forty-eight in midtown, and then the weekend looks great, one high pressure area will be leaving, another comes in. We don't see any storms, high temperatures both days around fifty-eight in midtown, warmer inland, cooler at the coast. Looking at Monday, increasing cloudiness, chance of rain later in the day and at night, high on Monday sixty. Currently in midtown forty-five degrees, the relative humidity sixty percent, winds out of the west at five miles per hour, forty-five heading for sixty-two.

It looks like a very nice day out there today, lots of sunshine, mild temperatures with a high getting up to near sixty degrees. It'll be clear to partly cloudy tonight, low slipping back to forty-six. Lots of sunshine again tomorrow, not as mild, but still pretty nice for this time of year, high of fifty-six. On Monday, morning sunshine, followed by increasing clouds, becomes windy, could be some rain late in the day, but more likely at night, high sixty-two. Then a partly sunny, breezy, cooler day for Tuesday, Tuesday's high only forty-eight. Currently fifty-three degrees at Newark, fifty-four degrees at LaGuardia, in Central Park lots of sunshine, fifty-two, relative humidity fifty-eight percent, and a variable wind at seven miles per hour. Repeating the current temperature fifty-two going up to near sixty in midtown.

Well, it may be late November, but these nice balmy temperatures will continue right through Monday. Today just beautiful, fifty-eight this afternoon with sunshine. Tonight, clear to partly cloudy, down to forty in the suburbs, forty-eight in midtown. Sun followed by clouds tomorrow, some rain at night, the high tomorrow near sixty. Then brisk and colder Tuesday and Wednesday, sunny to partly cloudy, highs in the upper-forties to low fifties. Everybody's wondering about Thanksgiving Day. Well, I think we're gonna see some rain for Turkey Day, especially in the afternoon. Now, right now we have forty-five in Morristown, forty-six in Islip, sunshine and forty-eight in Central Park, seventy-three percent humidity, east winds at eight, forty-eight right now, going up to fifty-eight today.

Clouds increasing after a beautiful weekend, and it does look like some rain on the way starting late afternoon or early evening, and then it'll rain for, ur, five or six hours during the night tonight, and clear up late tonight, turn blustery and chilly, though. Our high today up to fifty-nine, low tonight forty-two. Tomorrow a sunny day, but brisk and colder, the high forty-eight. Mostly sunny and seasonably chilly on Wednesday, the high of fifty. Then clouding up on Thanksgiving Day, with a chance of rain, hopefully late in the day, but we'll keep you posted on that. Forty-six and partly cloudy now in Central Park, humidity eighty-eight percent, wind out of the east at four. Again, the current temperature forty-six going up to fifty-nine today.

It will be chilly, but it will be sunny today with the temperature, uh, getting up to about forty-eight this afternoon, then it'll be clear and cold tonight, low middle-thirties, in the city but the twenties in most suburbs. Sunshine for the most part tomorrow, with a high near fifty. We get to Thanksgiving Day, we'll have thickening clouds, and then by the end of the day, some rain. But it looks like that rain will hold off long enough, we'll be able to get the, uh, parade festivities in, and by the time it starts to rain, most of us, uh, including yours truly, uh, may be asleep on the couch. And Friday is partly sunny, windy, and chilly again. Thirty-seven and sunny now in Central Park, humidity fifty-nine percent, wind out of the northwest, gusting to eighteen miles an hour. Again, the current temperature thirty-seven, going up to forty-eight today.

No snow. No rain. No fog. The three big dangers of travel this time of year, and that's the case up and down the eastern seaboard as it's a dry day, and also dry into most of the Midwest, afternoon temperature getting to fifty-two today, down to forty-four tonight. Tomorrow, clouds and sunny breaks, temperature forty-six around nine in the morning, then in the afternoon getting into the fifties, and it'll rain tomorrow night and Friday morning, becoming windy Friday afternoon with some clearing, high fifty-eight. And Saturday looks like a cold, blustery day, it'll feel like it's in the thirties all day with gusty, northwest winds. Currently thirty-seven degrees in midtown, relative humidity sixty-nine percent, wind northeast at five, thirty-seven heading for fifty-two.

Crowds are lining up already for the Macy's Thanksgiving Day Parade, temperature in an hour forty-six. It'll climb into the low to mid-fifties this afternoon, just a beautiful day, but then rain will be arriving overnight, and will last into tomorrow, and by this time tomorrow the, uh, the weather'll look, uh, a lot drippier than it'll be right underneath where the, uh, turkey is dripping into the pan today. Tomorrow's high fifty-eight degrees and Saturday, wind, much colder, intervals of clouds and sun, could be a flurry especially in the morning, high forty-six, the RealFeel temperature will be near freezing, and Sunday still windy with some sunshine, high forty-eight degrees. So a cold, but dry weekend coming up. Currently in midtown forty-three degrees, relative humidity sixty-seven percent, the air is calm. It's partly to mostly cloudy across the area, forty-three heading to fifty-four.

With the . . . between the rain and the fog today, it will be, uh, messy driving if you're driving about, uh, periods of rain continuing well into tonight, some of it heavy, the high this afternoon sixty. There is a dense fog advisory now for Bronx, The Queens, uh, The Bronx and Queens and all of Long Island, and up into Connecticut as well, so please be careful if you're driving. It's going to become windy and colder late tonight, with the low down near forty by daybreak, and then a rain or snow shower possible early tomorrow, very windy and colder, with some sun in the afternoon, winds gusting past forty miles per hour. So the high will reach forty-six, but the RealFeel temperature will only be thirty-two, degrees for a high tomorrow. Sunday, partly sunny and windy, high fifty. Monday, variably cloudy with a chilly wind, high forty-six. Tuesday, mostly sunny and chilly, high forty-two. Currently in midtown it's fifty-four degrees with light rain, relative humidity of one hundred percent, winds out of the south at nine, the barometer twenty-nine point eighty-three and falling. Repeating the temperature fifty-four going to a high of sixty today.

Strong winds have pushed the rain and warmth of the tri-states, uh, that we had yesterday well offshore, in fact, today's just going to be a very windy, chilly day with clouds and some sunshine, and it's a sprinkle, or even a flurry, our high forty-six. Those winds will gust over forty miles an hour at times. Tonight, partly cloudy, less wind, a low in the low to mid-thirties. A mix of sun and clouds on tap for tomorrow, a high near fifty. It'll become windy Monday with more sun than clouds, high forty-eight. Blustery and cold Tuesday, partly sunny skies, the high close to forty. Currently it's forty-three in Islip and at LaGuardia, forty-two and cloudy in Central Park, relative humidity fifty-seven percent, the wind out of the west at seven, gusting to twenty-three miles an hour. Repeating the current temperature forty-two going up to forty-six in midtown.

A windy day today, with a mix of clouds and sunshine. There's a slight chance for a sprinkle, uh, mid to late morning as a cold front approaches and passes through the area. And behind that, the wind will really kick up, could gust to between thirty and forty miles an hour this afternoon, and it will get colder tonight, with a low down near freezing in the city, and windy and cold with sunshine tomorrow, the high temperature tomorrow only thirty-six, and the RealFeel temperature will be well down into the twenties. Sunshine, less wind but still cold Wednesday and Thursday, and then increasing cloudiness on Friday. Right now it is forty-six and partly cloudy in Central Park, humidity fifty-three percent, southwest wind gusting to eighteen miles per hour. Again the current temperature forty-six going up to fifty today.

It's squalling in some neighborhoods, not everywhere, in fact, in most places it's either flurrying or, uh, not snowing at all, but we've had a couple of intense snow squalls. They don't last much more than ten minutes or so. One is now, uh, moving into, uh, Suffolk County east of Mineola and the other one, coming across the Bronx, it'll probably, uh, get to Flushing, uh, around Shea Stadium, in, uh, the next, uh, ten to twenty minutes. Then there'll be sunshine, uh, but the wind and the cold will be constant today, with the high in the middle-thirties. Then it's clear tonight, low near twenty. Sunny, less wind and cold tomorrow, increasing clouds Thursday and Friday, into the weekend. We may have to deal with a real nor'easter-type storm along the eastern seaboard, so keep in touch with us. Right now thirty-three and mostly cloudy in Central Park, humidity fifty-one percent, wind from the northwest at ten. Again the current temperature, thirty-three going up to thirty-six today.

Mostly sunny and cold today, going up to thirty-four, the RealFeel temperature this afternoon will be in the twenties. As a reference point, the real temperature right now is eleven. Clear and cold tonight, low twenty-six in midtown, fourteen in some suburbs. Tomorrow sunshine followed by clouds, high forty-two. Part one of a potential two-part storm would reach us on Friday, with some snow or rain arriving, high thirty-eight. The biggest part, assuming it develops, would be during the course of the weekend. We'll be very close to the snow-rain line and so it's impossible to estimate how much snow there could be, but it could be a disruptive storm throughout the region, in terms of travel, during the course of the weekend. Forty degrees our projected high, or thirty-eight on Saturday, and about the same on Sunday. Currently twenty-one degrees, relative humidity fifty-nine percent, wind west at eight miles per hour, twenty-one heading to thirty-four.

Fine weather for today, not much wind, the temperature rebounding from the recent chill, going to forty, thickening clouds tonight, low thirty-four. Now, we're predicting some snow spreading across the area between eight and noon tomorrow, then accumulating one to three inches along the coast, three to six inches inland. Does it have to happen? No. There are some indications the storm can weaken, never get here. We'll rate that about a one in four chance that nothing would actually happen tomorrow, but three out of four that something will, so we need to be ready for slippery places, and then a change to rain at the end of the day. Saturday, the storm will strengthen offshore, again, will it be close enough to the coast to give us a lot of snow and strong wind, or just offshore far enough that we don't get much precipitation at all? That is partly dependent on what happens to the first system. The high at that . . . Saturday, thirty-four, Sunday, an easier forecast, sunshine thirty-eight, Monday, sunshine thirty-six. Currently thirty-two degrees, relative humidity forty-nine percent, wind north at five, thirty-two heading for forty.

Well, we're continuing to watch snow sloat . . . spread slowly northward, uh, through New Jersey, uh, snowing around Trenton and, eh, Princeton, uh, not yet to Somerville, uh, or, a, to Belmar, but it probably begins there by about nine o'clock, uh, nine to ten o'clock into, uh, Manhattan by about noon. And then, a couple of hours after that, it'll spread across Long Island and into Connecticut. There can be rain mixed with the snow at times this afternoon and evening, but then the snow falls, uh, continuously later tonight, and into tomorrow morning, and we think we're gonna wind up with an average of three to six inches of snow across the metropolitan area with the, uh, six, perhaps, more favored than the three. And you go north and west of Interstate 287, there can be a foot of snow or more, before it tapers off later tomorrow. Right now thirty-three, just cloudy in Central Park, humidity eighty-eight percent, wind out of the northeast at nine. Again, the current temperature thirty-three, temperatures around freezing during the snow.

It is closing in again. Snowfall intensities picking up across the tri-state area, and we will have heavy snow through the, uh, day today and into, uh, part of tonight as well. The snowfall rates can be on the order of an inch, to even an inch to two inches per hour, on occasion. And, uh, we think by around midnight tonight, we'll have an average of twelve to eighteen inches of snow across the metropolitan area. And that does not include drifting, which is going to become more significant with time, because the wind will be picking up and, uh, that's the reason the blizzard warning is in effect. The combination of blowing snow and falling snow can create near visibilit . . . near zero visibilities on occasion. Twenty-five degrees and lightly snowing now, we're headed up to thirty in midtown.

Well, this storm winding down here as far as, uh, accumulating snow goes. Uh, there should be little accumulation from this point on and, uh, we will see, though, very strong winds continuing right on through the night. Uh, the center of this nor'easter only moving to about Cape Cod by morning, temperatures staying in the middle-twenties, uh, a lot of blowing and drifting in open areas. Uh, for tomorrow also very windy, cold, but, uh, we will see some sunshine returning, thirty-two in the afternoon. Monday a much more tranquil day, lots of sunshine, thirty-eight, mid-forties on Tuesday with sunshine. We may hit fifty on Wednesday as clouds come in ahead of the, uh, next frontal system, and that one will be delivering rain. In Central Park twenty-five degrees, light snow, we have a north wind twenty-five, gusting forty-five miles an hour. Repeating the current temperature twenty-five going down to twenty-three in midtown.

Well, our storm is over now, uh, all except for the melting which, uh, will begin a little bit this afternoon, then it'll freeze up tonight, with plenty of sun today, and temperatures getting above freezing this afternoon. There will be some melting, but tonight will be clear and cold, low twenty-six in the city, into the teens in the suburbs. Sunshine tomorrow, up to forty, that'll really start the melting. The problem is there'll be rain that comes along Wednesday afternoon and night, into part of Thursday, with temperatures getting into the forties, and that rain and thaw and melting snow could create some flooding problems Wednesday night and Thursday. Right now, twenty-five and, um, mostly clear in Central Park, humidity fifty-eight percent, wind northwest at seven. Again the current temperature twenty-five, going up to thirty-six.

Plenty of sunshine will be the rule, although at times there will be a deck of clouds that show up, so it's not going to be a totally sunny day, temperature today getting to about forty degrees. Partly to mostly cloudy tonight, low thirty-six in midtown, twenty-five to thirty in many of the colder suburbs. Then as we look at the day tomorrow, variable cloudiness, high forty-eight. Now, it's not out of the question if some drizzle breaks out early, as moist air comes in from the southeast, but rain will be with us tomorrow night, and that rain can be heavy. That, plus melting snow, can lead to flooding in, uh, poor drainage areas, lots of slush around. And Thursday afternoon, the rain's all gone, clouds breaking for sun, windy, high fifty-two. Then Friday partly sunny with a cold wind, high forty-six. Currently it's thirty-one and cloudy, relative humidity sixty-nine percent, winds out of the north at four miles per hour, thirty-one heading for forty.

Well, uh, back when we got the snowstorm over the weekend, that generated about two-thirds of an inch of liquid equivalent or, in other words, if it wasn't cold enough for snow, but had it rained, we would've had about two-thirds of an inch of rain. Now, uh, we're expecting just as much rain, if not a little more, maybe around an inch, Wednesday night and Thursday morning. So, with melting snow and, uh, just about as much if not more rain, well, you get the idea where I'm going with this. Uh, there will be, I think, areas of flooding, poor drainage areas, some side streets, uh, places with storm sewers that are clogged, and you're gonna have, uh, a little bit of flooding to deal with. There's one good thing about all this, it will be turning milder with temperatures later today in the mid-forties, holding nearly steady or rising Wednesday night, peaking at fifty-two Thursday, then we turn drier and colder again. Right now it's cloudy and thirty-seven, humidity seventy-two percent, the wind east at six miles per hour. Cloudy, thirty-seven, heading down to thirty-four.

Pretty nice day out there, of course the snow melting, it is slush and water, but variable cloudiness, high forty-eight. Overcast tonight into tomorrow morning with rain, it'll be heavy at times after midnight, with flooding in poor drainage areas, a combination of rain and melting snow likely to cause a mess for the morning commute, temperatures steady or rising overnight. Then later tomorrow, but not till after lunch, windy and mild, clouds may break for some sun, high fifty-two. Friday sunny with a cold wind, high forty-four, RealFeel temperature in the low thirties. Then for Saturday sunshine, high forty. Currently the winds are light and variable, the relative humidity sixty-five percent, forty-three degrees in midtown heading for forty-eight.

We are going to continue to get a wind-swept, heavy rain for at least the next few hours. Uh, we've had street and highway flooding that will continue to be an issue into the early afternoon, and that wind gusting to between thirty and forty miles an hour on occasion, making umbrellas hard to handle as well. At least it's mild, temperatures in the fifties. Late in the day it'll begin clearing up and turn colder. Tonight partly cloudy, blustery and cold, a low thirty-six. Sunshine tomorrow forty-four, sunshine on Saturday, cold, high thirty-eight, then clouding up Sunday, followed by the chance for some rain or snow. Fifty-six degrees and rainy now in Central Park, humidity one hundred percent, wind from the east gusting to twenty-seven miles an hour. Again, the current temperature fifty-six going up to fifty-nine today.

Skies will be clearing out as we go through the night, uh, a gusty northwest wind will continue, and temperatures will be in the low thirties by daybreak. High pressure heading in our direction, uh, from, uh, south central Canada, uh, will bring us a good deal of sunshine here the next couple of days and, uh, chillier weather, mid-forties tomorrow, only upper-thirties on Saturday. The next system we have to tangle with is currently dropping some rain down over Arizona. This will be, uh, spreading across Texas during the day tomorrow and the, uh, reach, eh, the rest of the Gulf states on the weekend, and start heading northeastward. Uh, we expect an increasing wind and, uh, uh, cloudy skies here on Sat . . . or Sunday, I should say, uh, with, uh, snow or sleet breaking out. Probably changing over to rain late in the day or during the evening, and that would continue on into Monday morning, high Sunday about thirty-six. We have forty-five degrees and a cloudy sky in Central Park, a northwest wind twenty-five, gusting forty to forty-five miles an hour. Repeating the current temperature forty-five going down to thirty-four in midtown.

Yesterday we had the teeming tarns, the rain, the flooding, warm air. Today, dry air, cold winds, and that's pretty much it, the high'll be forty-four, RealFeel temperature this afternoon in the low thirties. Partly cloudy to clear tonight, cold, winds diminishing early, low thirty in midtown, twenty-two to twenty-six most suburbs. Tomorrow, sunshine followed by cloudiness, high thirty-eight. Then it looks like a storm visits on Sunday, snow at first mixing with or changing to rain in the city, and elsewhere along the coast. Too early to tell whether there'll be any snow still on the ground at the end of the storm after the rain. In the northern and western suburbs, it may stay below freezing the whole time, and that could allow snow and ice with several inches accumulating. Monday the storm leaves, and it's dry into Tuesday. Currently, winds out of the west at ten, gusting to eighteen miles per hour, the relative humidity fifty-two percent, thirty-seven in midtown heading forty-four.

It'll be sunny to partly cloudy today, we'll have a high of thirty-eight degrees. Clouds increase, thicken and lower tonight, low falling back to thirty. Cloudy, increasingly windy, a cold day tomorrow, snow or sleet will begin during the morning hours. Pretty quick change over to rain in the afternoon, though, from New York City on to the southeast, one to three inches there. We . . . north of 180 . . . um, 287, I should say, however, we'll see a mixture continue most of the day, could see three to six inches of ice and snow by the end of the day, with a high of thirty-six. Maybe a little rain or drizzle will start the day Monday, otherwise mostly cloudy with a high of forty. Mostly sunny, warmer Tuesday, high forty-six. Currently in Central Park, thirty degrees, relative humidity fifty-nine percent, and a west wind at six miles per hour. Repeating the current temperature thirty going up to thirty-eight in midtown.

Well, uh, the wind is in the process of diminishing this Monday night, and because of that, well, it's gonna be a lot, uh, more tranquil around here late tonight and tomorrow. It should be a fairly sunny day, the nicest day of the week actually. We're headed down to thir-ty in midtown, twenty-five in most suburbs, highs tomorrow in the mid-forties. Clouds will roll in, though, tomorrow night and this'll be followed by periods of rain on Wednesday, some of which can be heavy, that's not good news, a weekend storm, then by Wednesday it rains. That seems to be the pattern the last two weeks. It'll be very windy in the wake of the rain on Thursday, with clouds and sun, Friday, temperatures near forty. It's clear and thirty-four in midtown right now, the humidity sixty-seven percent, wind west at twelve miles per hour gust-ing to eighteen. It's clear, thirty-four heading down thirty.

A nice day today. Sunshine will take temperatures up into the forties, and it'll be mild tonight but it will also cloud up, with a low near forty. Tomorrow our next storm begins to bring us rain, and rain tomorrow, and on into tomorrow night, will be heavy at times, could get an inch of rain, and that'll produce street and highway flooding. Inland areas, uh, the ground is saturated, uh, there's snow on the ground to melt, the rivers are high, and there's concern about river and stream flooding. And, in fact, flood watches are in effect in west-ern and northern suburbs, uh, for tomorrow and tomorrow night. Thursday, very windy, clouds break for some sun, maybe a few flurries around in the morning. Temperatures in the thirties and mostly sunny Friday, the high thirty-eight. Thirty-three and, uh, mostly sunny now in Central Park, humidity seventy-one percent, wind from the southwest at seven. Again, the current temperature thirty-three going up to forty-six today.

We've got rain west and north of the city. It will be raining, uh, by nine o'clock across most of the metropolitan area. The rain will be heavy and continue into this evening and street and highway flooding certainly can occur and, uh, with rivers and, uh, streams high in interior sections. There's also concern about that kind of flooding, and the flood watch is in effect for much of the area, our high today fifty-four. Turning windy and colder tonight, rain could end as a brief period of snow and flurries, the low thirty-four. Tomorrow partly sunny, very windy and cold, temperatures in the thirties. Partly sunny Friday, high thirty-eight, chance of flurries on Saturday. Right now it's fifty degrees and cloudy in Central Park, the rain still may be an hour or an hour and a half away, humidity one hundred percent, wind from the southeast at six. Again the current temperature fifty going up to fifty-four today.

Recently we've had storms every couple of days. One would be snow, one would be a mixture, one, like yesterday, would be all rain and wind. The big thing about the next five days is there aren't going to be any big storms, just cold, dry weather. Today's high thirty-nine, going down to thirty-two in midtown tonight, twenty-four in many suburbs, up to thirty-eight with some sun tomorrow, thirty-six on Saturday, maybe a flurry, Sunday partly sunny thirty-eight. Monday forty-two and we have time to, uh, make up some lost time on holiday shopping if, uh, any of those storms of previous weeks delayed you. Currently in midtown thirty-two degrees, relative humidity sixty percent, wind west at twelve, gusting to twenty, thirty-two heading to thirty-nine.

It looks like a fine weekend and, for outdoor activities, no problems. You can go skiing, go shopping, go nowhere, but the weather's going to be decent. We don't see any storms coming before Tuesday or Wednesday. For today, a mixture of clouds and sun, going to thirty-six. Partly cloudy tonight, low twenty-eight in midtown, twenty-two in some suburbs. Tomorrow, cloudy to partly sunny, brisk and cold, a flurry possibility, high thirty-six. Sunday, partly sunny, high thirty-six. Monday, not as cold, going to forty-six, and up to forty-eight, as clouds increase on Tuesday. Currently winds out of the west at five, relative humidity sixty-nine percent, thirty degrees in midtown heading for thirty-six.

Well, it looks like a quiet weekend if you're headed out to do some last-minute shopping for the holidays. You'll find cloudy to partly sunny skies, it'll be brisk and cold, with a stray flurry, and a high thirty-eight. Partly cloudy, cold tonight, down to twenty-five in midtown, twenty in the suburbs. Remember, tomorrow is the shortest day of the year, so we'll see times of sun and clouds, still cold, the high again tomorrow only thirty-eight. And we warm up on Monday, it'll be partly sunny with a high of forty-six. Increasing clouds on Tuesday, a high up to fifty, for Christmas Eve, windy with a chance for rain. Right now we have a temperature of thirty in Morristown, it's twenty-eight at Islip, and it's clear and thirty in Central Park, eighty percent humidity, a west wind at five. Thirty right now, headed up to thirty-eight this afternoon.

About the Author

Kenneth Goldsmith's writing has been called some of the most "exhaustive and beautiful collage work yet produced in poetry" by *Publishers Weekly.* The author of seven books of poetry, founding editor of the online archive UbuWeb (http://ubu.com), and the editor of *I'll Be Your Mirror: The Selected Andy Warhol Interviews,* Goldsmith is also the host of a weekly radio show on New York City's WFMU. He teaches writing at The University of Pennsylvania, where he is a senior editor of PennSound, a online poetry archive. More about Goldsmith can be found on his author's page at the University of Buffalo's Electronic Poetry Center: http://epc.buffalo.edu/authors/goldsmith.

Also by Kenneth Goldsmith

73 Poems (with Joan La Barbara)
No. 111 2.7.93-10.20.96
Fidget
Soliloquy
Head Citations
Day

EDITED BY KENNETH GOLDSMITH:
I'll Be Your Mirror: The Selected Andy Warhol Interviews